OUTLINE GRAMMAR

OF THE

SHAÍYANG MIRI LANGUAGE:

AS SPOKEN BY THE

MIRIS OF THAT CLAN RESIDING IN THE NEIGHBOURHOOD OF SADIYA

OUTLINE GRAMMAR

OF THE

SHAÍYANG MIRI LANGUAGE:

AS SPOKEN BY THE

MIRIS OF THAT CLAN RESIDING IN THE NEIGHBOURHOOD OF SADIYA

J. F. NEEDHAM

GYAN

Published by

GYAN

Gyan Publishing House
5, Ansari Road
Daryaganj, New Delhi-110002
Phone: 011-47034999, 9811692060
E-mail: books@gyanbooks.com

Distribution Network
gyanbooks.com
India, USA, Canada, UK, Australia

ISBN: 978-93-6780-067-6 (HB)

First Published, 1886

2nd Impression 2024

Printed at: Gyan Press, Delhi.

OUTLINE GRAMMAR OF THE SHAÍYÂNG MIRI LANGUAGE
Author: J. F. NEEDHAM

OUTLINE GRAMMAR

OF THE

SHAI'YÂNG MIRI LANGUAGE

AS SPOKEN BY THE

Miris of that Clan residing in the Neighbourhood of Sadiya.

WITH ILLUSTRATIVE SENTENCES, PHRASE-BOOK, AND VOCABULARY.

By J. F. NEEDHAM,

ASSISTANT POLITICAL OFFICER, SADIYA.

SHILLONG:
PRINTED AT THE ASSAM SECRETARIAT PRESS.

1886.

PREFACE.

THE Miris who reside on the banks of the Brahmaputra, Dihong, and Dibong rivers, in the neighbourhood of Sadiya, call themselves Mi'shing (I have not yet been able to find out the derivation of the word), and are of the Shai'yâng,* Oi'yân,* Chû-ti'yâ,† Dâm'bûk,* and Shôm'wâng clans, each of which is divided into numerous sub-divisions.

They are not of themselves a numerous body, inasmuch as their whole community is under 1,500 souls, but there can be no doubt that they are closely allied to the Miris residing lower down the Brahmaputra, as also to the numerous tribe of hill Miris in North Lakhimpur, and I know that their language is in most respects similar to that spoken by those Miris, for in December 1883 some Sadiya Miris (who were accompanying me to the Calcutta Exhibition) landed at Nigriting, and in conversation with the Miris residing there, appeared to be as thoroughly at home as they would have been amongst their own people at Sadiya, while that of the first four clans mentioned is almost word for word the same as that spoken by the Bor Abors, a numerous (we know of some 20,000 people of this tribe, and we are aware that there are undoubtedly very many more to the north again of those we know of) and powerful tribe inhabiting the hills immediately to the north of Sadiya, between the Dihong and Dibong rivers, as also very closely, if not quite, similar to that spoken by the Pâ'si' and the Mi'nyôngs, two other numerous cognate tribes inhabiting the hills to the west (right bank) of the Dihong, and, such being the case, there can be no doubt that the compilation of a Grammar, however rudimentary and incomplete it may be, coupled with a

* The Assamese call these clans Shai-âng'yâ, Oi-ân'yâ, and Dâm-bûk'yâ, respectively.

† This is an Assamese word, including several clans [the chief of which are known (to the Miris) as Pâgrâ and De'lû] who have been settled in the plains of Assam for generations.

Vocabulary and a Phrase-book, appertaining to a language so widely spoken, is likely to prove useful, as also interesting and instructive, philologically. For these reasons, therefore, I have been tempted to record what little I have already learnt of the Miri-Abor language during my two and a half years' residence at Sadiya, lest in this uncertain world of ours something should transpire to prevent my doing so later on, for, having transcribed what I have already learnt, I may, if necessary hereafter, be able to revise, or add to, the work.

The work, unpretending though it be, has not been accomplished without difficulties, the chief being (*a*) my own, and, for that matter, most Miris also, imperfect knowledge of Assamese, which rendered it a difficult matter for me to explain thoroughly the points upon which I most wished for information; (*b*) the nearest Miri village being some five miles or so distant from Sadiya, I was prevented from mixing as freely, or as frequently, with the people as I should have wished. while for three or four months during the rains communications with them were virtually closed; (*c*), the fact that, although each clan possesses many different words to express the same meaning. they are so accustomed to mix one up with the other that it is a real difficulty to ascertain for certain what word should be used for a particular thing by a particular clan.

In this work, I have attempted to give an outline of the Shai′yâng Miri dialect, inasmuch as it is, if anything, more closely allied to Abor than the others, but I have no doubt that I have unavoidably, for the reasons given above, here and there used words which are not exclusively Shai′yâng.

In conclusion, I beg gratefully to acknowledge having received valuable assistance, in the shape of copious notes and suggestions, from E. Stack, Esq., C.S., without which this little work would have been far less full and complete than it now is.

J. F. Needham,

August 1885. *Assistant Political Officer, Sadiya.*

OUTLINE MIRI GRAMMAR.

PART I.—ORTHOGRAPHY.

As far as practicable I have followed the system of transliteration advocated by C. J. Lyall, Esq., C.S., C.I.E., in his admirable Note on "Language" drawn up in September 1881.

1. Vowels.

(a) when not marked always short, as in comp*a*ny, &c.

(â) long, as in *a*h, f*a*ther, &c.

N.B.—There are a few words in which this letter occurs, which it will be as well to notice here, *viz.*, in "pâ'to-kâ" =*strike* (in a horizontal manner) or *cut*, and in "pâ'to" =*received* (this last word sounds very Assamese, but it is regularly used by both Miris and Abors). The "â" in both words is identically the *same*, and the *first syllable* in *both* is accented, though a little less stress is required on the one in the *first* word. For instance, the "pâ" in "pâ-to'kâ"=*strike* is pronounced like the *pa* in the French word *patois*, while that in "pâ'to"=*received* is pronounced like *par* in such words as *pardon*, *partake*.

Again the "â" in the "kâ" in "kâ mâ," "kâ mâng,"=*not any*, *none*, is the same as that in "kâ"=*see* (root of verb), but the "â" in the two first mentioned kâ' requires less stress laid upon them than the one in "kâ"=*see*.

(å) like the sound of *a* in b*a*ll, &c.

(e) unmarked, like the *e* in th*e*n, m*e*t, b*e*d, &c.

(ê) like *ey* in th*ey*, or the *ai* in *ai*m.

(i) unmarked, like the *i* in p*i*n, *i*n, &c.

(î) like *i* in mach*i*ne, mar*i*ne, &c.

(o) unmarked, like the *o* in b*o*nd, n*o*t, &c.

(ô) like long *o* in b*o*ne, d*o*e, r*o*e, ye*o*man, &c.

(u) unmarked, like *u* in b*u*ll, &c.

(û) like the long sound of *oo* in pröve, dö, tömb, &c.

(ü) like the French *u* in l'*u*ne.

(ya) like the *u* in f*u*me, exh*u*me, or *ou* in y*ou*, &c.

Diphthongs.

(au) like *ow* in h*ow*, &c.
(ai) like the *i* in sh*i*ne, &c.
(oi) like the *oi* in b*oi*l, *oi*l, &c.
(ua) This sound is a peculiar one. It, however, only occurs in one word, *viz.*, "in'qua?" = *what*, the "qua" in which is pronounced more like the *qui* in "quirk" = *retort, &c.*, than anything else I can think of.
(ui) like the *ui* in the French word *ap'pui* (*point d'appui*). When not a proper diphthong, the vowel to be sounded is marked.

N.B.—*ui* is often pronounced differently by different Miris. For instance "mui" = *desire, wish*, is sometimes pronounced "mui," at others "mu'ĭ," and I have even heard it pronounced very like the *mur* in *murder*: "bui" = *he* is similarly pronounced "bui," "buî," or "bur'ĭ."

(ia) this is an improper diphthong, and the vowel (or vowels) to be sounded is marked.

2. Consonants.

(b) as in English.
(c) only used in conjunction with *h* when the *ch* should be pronounced like the *ch* in *ch*air.
(d) like the Sanskrit ব.
(g) hard, as in gun.
(h) as in English.
(j) as in joy.
(k) as in English.

N.B.—In a few words in which *k* occurs some letter is often colloquially omitted; as "ngåk bui'rå" = *my brother*, for "ngå'ka bui'rå." Again "ngôm å'kå bî'kå" is *give me one*, but the "kå" in "bî'kå" is generally *omitted*, thus "ngôm å'kå bî."

(l), (m), (n) as in English.

(ng) the nasal *n* in conjunction with *g* is *initial* in a few words; as, "ngå" = I (the Khásias have, I believe, the same word for I), "ngôm-nå'mü" = noise, &c. The *ga* in "ngå" is pronounced like the *ga* in *gall*, and to this sound must be added that of the nasal *n*.

When at the end of a word *ng* is pronounced like the *ng* in *king*, *sing*, &c.

N.B.—Words *ending* in *ng* often *drop* these two letters in conversation. For instance, the word for *village* is "då'lûng," but, "whose village is this?" would be—

sî då'lû sî se'ka då-lûng'a?*
this village this whose village?

Again, the stern of a boat is "kûng'kông," but "Put it in the stern" would be--

ê'lûng kûng-kô 'lâ ma'to-kâ.
boat stern in put.

so "long"=*a day*, but when used in conjunction with a numeral the *ng* is often dropped, as "lô-nyî'kå"=two days, &c.

(p) as in English.
(q) ditto.
(r) like the cerebral Hindustani *r*.

N.B.—There is often a perceptible roll to this letter when final, as in "tâ'kâr"=leopard, "dô'muir"=thunder, "â'muir"=body (human), &c.

(s) as in this.
(sh) as in *sh*all.
(t) like the Bengali ত.
(r) } as in English.
(y) }

3. Accent.

I do not think I can do better than follow the plan adopted by the Revd. Mr. Endle in his Kachari Grammar for marking the accented syllable, or syllables, of words.

The accented syllable in short words, therefore, I have marked with the acute (′) accent, while in words having two accented syllables I have used the double mark (″) for the *main*, and the single (′) for the *secondary* accent.

As the Miri language is, however, essentially a syllabic one, and abounds in intonations, I have also placed a hyphen between such syllables as have not been marked as above, and it must be understood that a slight modulation of the voice is required while each syllable so separated is being uttered.

General Rules relating to Accent.

The stress of the voice nearly always rests on the penultimate syllable of a word, as will be seen from what follows.

---

* Nominatival *a*.

1. *Nouns.*—The majority of these are dissyllabic; as, "mî′ma′ "=woman, "lê′pô"=foot, "â′lê"=leg, "po′rok" =fowl, "pô′lô"=moon, &c., and the accent is always on the first syllable, even though some of them may have a short vowel in the first, and a long vowel in the second syllable, but when their case endings are added, the accent is shifted to the second syllable; as—

mî-ma′ma=to a woman.
mî-ma′em=a woman (acct. case).

If the case ending is a double one, as in the ablative "ka′lok"=from, the accent is again shifted so as to fall on the penultimate syllable; as—

mî-ma-ka′lok=from a woman.

If the noun is a trissyllabic one the accent falls on the second (*penultimate*) syllable when the noun is in its simplest form; as, "men-dâ′rî"=a cat, "kô-pî′âng"=buttock, and when the case endings are added, it is again shifted on to the penultimate syllable; as—

men-dâ-rî′em=a cat (acct. case).
kô-pî-âng′lâ=on the buttock.

2. *Verbs.*—Root verbs of one syllable retain the accent on that syllable throughout the present and perfect definite tenses of the indicative mood, and the simple future (*i.e.*, so long as the tense suffixes are words of one syllable), but throughout the remaining tenses the accent is transferred to the first syllable of the tense suffixes; as—

ngâ kâ-tû′ai=I saw.
—— kâ-dûng′ai=I was seeing.
—— kâ-veg′dâ=I can see.
&c. &c.

Verbs with dissyllabic roots have the accent on the second syllable; as—

shâ-mân′to-kâ=play.
dur-jî′to kâ=dive.

and in compound verbs the second member of the compound takes the accent; as—

lû-bî′to-kâ=explain (lû=speak, bî=give).
gê-kî′to-kâ=try on clothes (gê=wear, ki=measure.)

Exception 1.—Root verbs of one syllable when in the imperative mood ending in "to-kâ" (pronounced exactly like the Assamese word টকা=rupee) as also when they have the prohibitive negative particle "yô-kâ"=don't, attached to them take the accent on the root. If the verbal root is a dissyllabic one, or the verb is a compound one, it rests on the second syllable or on the second member of the compound, as the case may be; as—

gi'to-kâ=go.
gi'yô-kâ=don't go.
shâ-mân'to-kâ=play.
shâ-mân'yô-kâ=don't play.
lû-bi'to-kâ=explain.
lû-bi'yô'-kâ=don't explain.

2. Adjectives in the comparative degree take the accent on the last syllable; as—

ai-yâ'=better.
bâ-dâ-yâ'=longer.
&c., &c.

When the imperative ends in "lâng'kâ"=go (later on, Assamese "jâ'bi") the accent again falls on the penultimate syllable; as—

gi-lang' ka=go.
shâ-mân-lâng'kâ=play.
lû-bî-lâng'kâ=explain.
&c., &c.

PART II.—ACCIDENCE.

I. Nouns.

1. *Gender.*

1. Nouns denoting inanimate objects have no formal distinction of gender.

2. Gender in the case of individuals of the human family is (with one or two exceptions to be noted hereafter) denoted (*a*) by different words, (*b*) by adding the word "mi'lông" (often abbreviated to "mi'lô")=male (human being) for the masculine, and "mi'ma=female (human being) for the feminine, to the noun; as—

(*a*) Examples.

Masculine.	*Feminine.*
Â'bû=father (when spoken of).	Â'na=mother (when spoken of.)
Bâ'bû= „ (when called).	Nâ'na= „ (when called).
Tâ'tô=grandfather, or great-grandfather.	Yai'ô=grandmother or great-grandmother.
Au=son.	Ô'ma=daughter.
Ô'ma mâk'bô=son-in-law.	Yâ-mung'ü=daughter in-law.

Masculine.	*Feminine.*
Mâk'bô=brother in-law.*	Ma'mô=sister in-law.*
Yî'gâ = ditto.	Ying'na=ditto.
Bui'râ=brother.	Buir' ma=sister.
" cousin.	" cousin.
Mî'lông=man, male (human being, also husband).	Mî'ma=female (human being) woman.
	Me'ang=wife.
Yâ'mê=young man.	Mî'ûm=young woman.
Â'kü=maternal uncle (also father-in-law).	(Same as mother)=maternal uncle.
Bâ'bû *or* Pai=paternal ditto.	Nyâ' nyî=paternal, aunt (also mother-in-law).
Mû'jing=old man.	Ur'jâ=old woman.

(*b*) EXAMPLES.

Masculine.	*Feminine.*
Kô mî-lông'kâ† *or*=child, male. mî-lô'kâ	Kô mî-ma'kâ†=child, female.
Rû'tûm mî-lông'kâ=master.	Rû'tûm mî-ma'kâ=mistress.
Tûm'bô mî-lông'kâ=widower.	Tûm'bô mî-ma'kâ=widow.

N.B.—Tûm'bô is equivalent to the Assamese word "bâ'ri," which is used, I believe, for widower and widow.

3. In the case of the inferior animals, gender is distinguished (*a*) by certain suffixes, with the reduplication of the last syllable of the noun (there are no monosyllabic words for animals), *viz.*, "bâ" for the masculine (which is occasionally changed without any apparent reason, unless for the sake of euphony, for "pâ," "râ," "vâ," and "tûm") and "na" for the feminine; (*b*) by adding "â-bâ'kâ†"=a male (animal) for the masculine, and "â-na'kâ"=a female (animal) for the feminine to the common noun; as—

(*a*) EXAMPLES.

	Masculine.	*Feminine.*
Ê'kî =dog.	Êkî kî'bâ.	Ê'kî kî'na.
Si'bê " monkey.	Si'bê bê'vâ.	Si'bê bê'na.
Si'râ‡ " pig, wild.	Si'râ râ'bâ.	Si'râ râ'na.
Si'râm " otter.	Si'râm râm'bâ.	Si'râm râm'na.
Si'tâ " elephant.	Si'tâ tâ'bâ.	Si'tâ tâ'na.
Si'tûm " bear.	Si'tûm tûm'râ.	Si'tûm tûm'na.

* A woman's husband calls all brothers older than his wife "mâk'bô," and they call him "yîgâ." If the wife has no brothers older than herself, her brothers call her husband "mâk'bô," and he calls them "yî'gâ."

† kâ=indefinite article *a* in English.

‡ Often pronounced "shi'râ."

	Masculine.	Feminine.
Shá'ben = goat.	Sha'ben ben'bâ.	Shâ'ben ben'na.
Tá'dê „ peacock.	Ta'dê dê'bâ.	Ta'dê dê'na.
Tâ'kâr „ leopard.	Tâ'kâr kâr'bâ.	Tâ'kâr kâr'na.
Ur'sâ „ mithon.	Ur'sâ sa'bâ.	Ur'sâ sa'na.
Po'rôk „ fowl, domestic.	Po'rôk rôk'pâ.	Po'rôk rông'na.
Pa'shin „ „ wild.	Pa'shin shin'pâ.	Pa'shin shin'na.

In some instances some letter in the last syllable of the common noun is changed (probably for the sake of euphony) ere the suffix is appended; as—

(*a*) Examples.

	Masculine.	Feminine.
Ê'ek = pig, tame.	Ê'ek e*r*'bâ.	Ê'ek e*r*'na.
Pa'jâp. „ duck.	Pa'jâp jâ*b*'bâ.	Pa'jâp jâ*m*'na.
Men'jâk „ buffalo.	Men'jâk jâk-tûm.	Men'jâk jâ*ng*'na.
Sá'rôk „ rhinoceros.	Sa'rôk rôk'tûm.	Sá'rôk rô*ng*'na.
Sim'yâ „ tiger.	Sim'yâ *nyă*'bâ.	Sim'yâ *nyă*'na.
Kê'bûng „ mouse, or rat.	Kê'bûng b*ă*'bâ.	Kê'bung b*ă*'na.

The instances in which these suffixes are used to distinguish the sex of a human being occur in the following words:—

Masculine.		Feminine.	
Pâk'bâ	= slave.	Pâng'na.	= slave.
Tûm'bâ mî-long'kâ *	„ widower.	Tûm'bâ nî-ma'kâ.	„ widow.

(*b*) Examples.

		Masculine.	Feminine.
Si'mon	= deer (generally)	Simon â-bâ'kâ ‡	Si'mon â-na'kâ ‡.
Ming-shâ'ron	„ jackal.	Ming-shâ'ron „	Mingshâ ron „
Tâ'bui	„ snake.	Tâbui „	Tâ'bui „
Gô'rû †	„ cow.	Gôrû „	Gôrû „

and similarly all other animals, birds, &c., not enumerated above under (*a*) or (*b*) examples.

If the question, "Is it a male or female?" had to be asked with reference to any of the animals mentioned under (*a*) examples, it would, with reference to a dog, for instance, be—

Kî-bâ'yü § kî-na'yü ? §
dog male dog female ?

and if with reference to any of those under (*b*) examples—

â-bâ-kâ' yü ? § â-na-kâ'yü ? §
male ? female ?

* *kă* equivalent to English indefinite article *a*.
† Miris have no word for cow.
‡ This "kâ" is equivalent to the indefinite article *a*.
§ Interrogative alternative particle.

2. *Number.*

The plural of nouns may be formed by the use of the suffix "kî′ding" often abbreviated to "kî′dî," but it is, as a rule, only used to denote a large number. It is used with all nouns.

EXAMPLES.

Kô kî-ding′a * shâ-mân′dûng. Children playing are	The children are playing.
Sim † ât′târ kî′dî sim † bôm-kâ·lâng kâ. These things these take away.	Take those things away.

3. *Case.*

1. The nominative, possessive, dative, and accusative cases appear to have genuine case-endings, though they are occasionally omitted, probably owing to carelessness of speech, while the ablative (which includes the instrumental) and loc. cases are formed by post positions.

2. The nominative is known by the affix "a" as also by its position as the first word in a sentence. When the noun is qualified, the "a" is omitted; as—

EXAMPLES.

Ê-kî′a ngôm rek′tô. Dog me bitten has	A dog has bitten me.
Mî′ûm kî-ding′a mâk′shâ shâ′dûng Young women dancing are	The young women are dancing.
A-mi′kâ â-si′lâ′ ô-lek′kâng A man water in fallen	A man has fallen into the water.
Du′mai bui ngôm gâ·sor′em bi′tô Dumai he me cloth given has	Dumai gave me a cloth.

3. The possessive is known by the affix "ka." It is, however, used peculiarly as the *possessive* genitive, and hence chiefly with the names of human beings.

Where the genitive is as much a genitive of *quality* as of *possession* "ka" may be, and usually is, omitted; and where a shade of either sense is discernible (and there are, of course, plenty of such cases) "ka" can be used, or omitted, according to taste.

EXAMPLES.

Si ngâ′kâ bâ-bû′ka ê-kûm′a. * This my father's house.	This is my father's house.
Si dâ′lû si sê-ka dâ-lûng′a? * This village this whose village? Dû-mai′ka. Dumai's.	Whose house is this? It is Dumai's.

* Nominatival *a*.

† Demonstrative pronoun, accusative case.

Ngâ Du-mai'ka au'a * I Dumai's son.	I am Dumai's son.
Â-nü'ka gâ-sôr'a* koi-â'dûk. Mother's cloth dirty is.	Mother's cloth is dirty.
Du-mai'ka kâng-kâ'lâ bî'to-kâ. Dumai sight in give.	Give it in the presence of Dumai.
Min-dâ'rî âm-wit'a. * Cat hair.	Cat hair (sense of quality).
Min-dâ-rî'ka âm-wit'a. * Cat hair.	Cat's hair (sense of possession).
É'ek â'lê ân-dû dûk. Pig leg shor are.	Pig's legs are short.

4. The dative is marked by the affix "ma"; as—

EXAMPLES.

Du-mai'ma bî'to-kâ. Dumai to give.	Give it to Dumai.
Ur-jâ' ma len-kân'to'-kâ. Old woman to show.	Show it to the old woman.
Ngâ nâ-nü' ma gâ-sôr'kâ bî'tô I mother to cloth given have.	I gave mother a cloth.
Dû-mai' ma sâ gi-â'lâng" kâ em'to-kâ. Dumai to here come say.	Tell Dumai to come here.

"em," the accusative case affix, is also used to mark this (dative) case, but only with the verb to give. This verb, in fact, governs a double accusative; as—

EXAMPLES.

Po'rôk au'em âm'buin bi-lâng' kâ. Fowl young to rice give.	Give the chickens some rice.
Ngâ ngâ' ka bui-râ' em bî' tô. I my brother to given have.	I gave it to my brother.
Dong'kâl sim† pa'jâp kîdî' dem yop-bî' to-ka. Worm this ducks to throw.	Throw this worm to the ducks.
Â'mî kî' dî dem† bî' tô. Men to given have.	I gave it to the men.

5. The accusative is marked by the affix "em," and is generally placed immediately before the active verb; as—

EXAMPLES.

Dû'mai bui mî-ma'em pâ'tô. Dumai he woman struck.	Dumai struck a woman.
Dû'mai bui âb-bûk'em re'pü mui-dûng' ai. Dumai he gun buy will wishing was.	Dumai wanted to buy a gun.

---

* Nominatival *a*.

† Demonstrative pronoun, accusative case.

Em-pû'em bôm-â'lâng"kâ. Mat bring.	Bring a mat.
Bui Pâ'dâm dà-lû'là âm-buin'em rê-kâ pü gî'kâng. He Abor village to rice buy purpose of gone.	He has gone to an Abor village to buy rice.
Kî-chûng'em tû' yô-kâ. Pup , kick not.	Do not kick the pup.

6. The ablative in its sense of *from the possession of*, *from the time of*, *from the locality of*, is formed by the genitival "ka," and the postposition "lok" (=from)="ka'lok," to which a second "ka" * is often added, apparently for no other reason than the sake of euphony; as—

EXAMPLES.

Ngâ Dû-mai-ka' lok" ka pâ' tô. I Dumai from received.	I got it from Dumai.
Bui ma-lô-ka' lok" ka kî'kâng *or* kî'dûng. He yesterday from ill became.	He has been ill since yesterday.
Bui Dî'brû ba-lok'† ka bôm'tûng. He Dibru there from brought.	He brought it from Dibrugarh.
Bui a-lok'‡ ka kâ'pü bôm-â-dû'na? § He there from what bringing is?	What is he bringing from yonder.
Ñgâ Dû-mai-ka' lok" ka lâ' pü. I Dumai' from take will.	I will take it from Dumai.
Sâk'ka gî-gê-kâng'kâ. This place from go.	Go hence.

In interrogative sentences the euphonic "ka" is omitted, and it is likewise omitted in sentences which contain a verb of command; as—

EXAMPLES.

Sim gâ'sôr sim nâ'ka nâ-na-ka' lok pâ-tô'na?§ This cloth this your mother from received have?	Did you get this cloth from your mother?
Dû-mai-ka'lok mûr'kông bâr‖-pî kâ lâ-bi¶ tô-î" kâ. Dumai from rupee four bring (and) give.	Bring four rupees from Dumai, and give me.

* It may be merely "a," but it is oftener pronounced as an extra "ka."

† Ba' la=a place *down* stream.

‡ A' la=there in sight.

§ Interrogative of verb.

‖ Bâr=numerical particle.

¶ Lâ-bî 'to-i "kâ=Assamese â-nî 'â dî'bî (lâ=take, bî=give).

When persons are not concerned, the genitival "ka" is omitted; as—

EXAMPLES.

Bâ-zâr'lok bôm-ê'lâng'kâ. Bázár from bring.	Bring it from the bázár.
Nâ bâ'zâr' lok pâ-tô' yü?* You bázár from get have?	Did you get it from the bázár?
Ê-kum' lok oi' to-ka. House from down come.	Come down from the house.
Ngâ-lû' ka â-pông'a† âm-buin'lok mô' dâk. Our liquor rice from made is.	Our liquor is made from rice.
Ngâ ô-ying'em yûm-râ lok tâ' dâ. I vegetables jungle from bring.	I get vegetables from the jungle.
Ngâ sim â'gôm sim dâ' lûng â-mi' lok tât' tô. I these words these village people from heard have.	I heard this story from the villagers.

7. The ablative postposition "lok," is also used to denote the *instrumental* case; as—

EXAMPLES.

Dû'mai bui mi-ma'em û-kâ' lok pâ' tô Dumai he woman stick with strike has	Dumai struck a woman with a stick.
Nâ buim û-kâ'lok pâ-tô-na'yü?‡ â-lâk' lok pâ-tô-na'yü?‡ You him stick with strike have? hand with strike have?	Did you strike him with a stick or with (your) hand?
Gâ-sôr'lok tid-buin'to-kâ. Cloth with wipe.	Wipe it with a cloth.
Sî mon â'sik dem yôk-shik'lok dî' to-kâ.§ Deer skin it knife with skin.	Skin the deer with a knife.

N.B.—As there is no passive voice in Miri, the case of the agent cannot be formed.

"Lok" is also used, in the sense of *by*, *through*, to denote direction; as—

EXAMPLES.

Bui yüm-râ'lok gî'kâng. He jungle through gone.	He has gone through the jungle.

* Interrogative of verb.
† Nominatival "a."
‡ Interrogative of verb.
§ Â'sik dî 'tokâ=skin an animal.

Men'jâk ki'dî da * ê-tôr'lok dûk'kâng. Buffaloes they fence through ran away.	The buffaloes ran off through the fence.
Â-sî'em pü'nem tem-pü'lok ân-jâ'kâ Water than road from little mô-tê-yâ' † dâk farther is	It is a little farther by road than by water.
Dû'mai'ka dâ-lûng'a ‡ yôd'dûng, Dumai village tabooing, Sê-kô' tê dâ-lû' lok gî-pâ' mâ.§ anyone at all villlage through go must not.	Dumai village is tabooing, no one can pass through it.

and lastly "lok" is used to denote the *means by which* locomotion is made; as—

EXAMPLES.

Bui si-tâ'lok gî'âng-kâ. He elephant by came	He came by elephant.
Nâ ê-lû lok gî-dâng-na'yü ? â-lê'lok You boat by came? feet by gî-dâng-na'yü? came?	Did you come by boat, or did you walk?
Â'sî ai'rup tôr-gâ'lok bui ê-lû'lok Water very strong consequently he boat by shâ‖ la'mâ come upstream able not	He cannot come by boat because the water is very strong.

8. The Loc. is formed by the postposition "lâ"¶; as—

EXAMPLES.

Â-mi'kâ â-si'lâ ô-lek'kâng Man a water in fallen has	A man has fallen into the water.
Nâ'ka ê-gin'lâ in'qua dû'na ?** Your basket in what is ?	What is in your basket ?
Dâ-nyî'lâ ma'to-kâ Sun in put	Put it in the sun.
Bui ê-kum'lâ dûng He house in is	He is in the house.
M mak lâ buim pâtô	He was killed in battle.
Nâ'ka gôg-dâ'dem ngâ yüm-râ'lâ dûng'ai Your calling whilst I jungle in was	I was in the jungle when you called.
Bui ê-lû'lâ gî'kâng He boat in went	He went in a boat.

---

* da=demonstrative pronoun.
† yâ=sign of comparative degree.
‡ Nominatival *a*.
§ gî-pâ'mâ=wrong to go: Assamese "jâ'bô" nâ pai'.
‖ shâ'to-kâ=go upstream.
¶ The postposition "lâ" means at, in, or into, to or unto, on or upon, by or near to.
** Interrogative of verb.

"lâ" is also used to denote motion towards a place; as—

EXAMPLES.

Bui ê-kum'lâ gi'kâng He house to gone has	He has gone to the house.
Nâ a-di'lôg pui*-gâ'lâ gi'pui'â ?† You when "ghát" to go will ?	When will you go to the ghát.

"lâ" is also used, in conjunction with the genitival "ka" to denote (*a*) *motion towards persons*, (*b*) *accompaniment* when *persons* are concerned; as—

(*a*) EXAMPLES.

Bui-ka'lâ gi-kâ'lâng"kâ His side to go	Go to him (*i.e.*, to the side of).
Nâ Dû-pû-ri-ka'lâ gi-pui'â? You Dupuri side to go will ?	Will you (child address-ed) go to Dupuri ?

(*b*) EXAMPLES.

Kâm'ti â-pi'kâ ngâ-ka'lâ Câl-kâ-tâ'lâ gi-muin'kâ ‡ Khamptis four me with Calcutta to went	Four Khamptis accompa-nied me to Calcutta.
Nâ bui-ka'lâ gi-muin‡ pui'â ?§ You his (person) with accompany will ?	Will you accompany him ?

If the plural termination be used, the genitival "kâ" is omitted; as—

EXAMPLE.

Á'mi ki-di'lâ gi'yo-kâ Men with go not	Do not go with the men.

The genitival "ka" is likewise omitted when persons are not concerned; as—

EXAMPLES.

Bui ê-lû'lâ gi'kâng He boat with gone	He has gone with the boat.
Si'râ au ki'di da‖ â-na'lâ â-gin'pü gi-muin'‡ dâ Pig (wild) young they mother with always accompany	Young pig always accom-pany their mother.
Yûm'râ men-jâk'a¶ tâ'ni men-jâk'lâ yê'$ muin mâ Jungle buffaloes tame buffaloes with remain not	Wild buffaloes do not re-sort with tame ones.

---

* "pui"=fill water, "gâ"=place.

† the *i* in "pui" is euphonic.

‡ "muin"=comitative particle.

§ Interrogative of verb.

‖ "da"=demonstrative pronoun.

¶ Nominatival a.

$ yê'to-kâ=reside, or live, somewhere.

And, lastly, "lâ" is used, in conjunction with the genitival "ka" (which is, however, then pronounced "kâ," apparently for the sake of euphony) to denote in the presence, sight, or hearing of, a person; as—

EXAMPLES.

Ngâ mûr kông'em bui'ka kâng-kâ'lâ bî'tô I rupee his presence in gave	I gave the rupee in his presence.
Bû'lû bui'ka tât-kâ'lâ lû'tô They his hearing in said	They said it in his hearing.
Ngâ â'mî kî'ding tât-kâ'lâ lû to I men hearing of said	I said it in the hearing of the men.
Koi-âng-kâ'na* gâ-sôr'em gê'lâ Dirty clothes wearing Sâ-heb'ka kâng-kâ'lâ gi'yô-kâ Saheb's presence in go not	Do not go in the saheb's presence wearing dirty clothes.

The above might be equally correctly rendered by using "kâ dôm" and "tât'dôm" for "kâng-kâlâ'" and "tât-kâlâ;" as—

Ngâ mûr-kông'em bui'ka kâ 'dôm bî'tô
I rupee his sight given have
&c. &c.

Abstract nouns cannot be formed in Miri.

4. II.—ADJECTIVES.

1. Adjectives have three degrees of comparison, *viz.*, positive, comparative, and superlative; as—

EXAMPLES.

Positive.	*Comparative.*	*Superlative.*
Ai ... good	Ai-yâ' ... better	Â-pui'lok ai-yâ' best (lit. all from best).
Ai'mâ ... good not (bad)	Ai-yâ'mâ ... good, more not (worse).	Â-pui'lok ai-yâ' mâ good, all from not good.
Kân'kân . pretty.	Kân-kân-yâ' prettier.	Â-pui'lok kân-kân-yâ. prettiest.
Bat'tê ... large.	Bat-tê-yâ'... larger.	Â-pui' lok bât-tê-yâ. largest.
Bâ'dâ ... long.	Bâ-dâ-yâ' ... longer.	Â-pui' lok bâ-dâ-yâ. lo ngest.

* "Koi-âng'kâ'na" means "possessed of dirty!" The "na" is the adjectival "na" noticed at page 16 *post.*

Positive.	*Comparative.*	*Superlative.*
Mô'tê ... far.	Mô-tî-yâ' ... farther.	Â-pui'lok mô-tê-yâ'. farthest.
Â'mê ... young.	Â-mê-yâ' ... younger.	Â-pui'lok â-mê-yâ'. youngest.
Mûjî ... old.	Mû-jî-yâ' ... older.	Â-pui'lok mû-jî-yâ'. eldest.

N.B.—"Gâm," an intensive particle signifying *middling, somewhat, little,* is generally tacked on to the positive form in order to temper or attenuate its force; as—

EXAMPLES.

Gâ-sôr'a	ân-jâ'kâ	ai-gâm' dâk	The cloth is a somewhat good one.
Cloth	somewhat (middling)	good is	

2. The comparative degree is generally used when the qualified noun is compared with another noun singly with regard to the same quality.

It is formed by putting the noun compared in the accusative case and inserting the conjunction "pü'num" = than after it, and adding the comparative adjectival sign "yâ" to the positive degree of the adjective; as—

EXAMPLES.

Ngâ'ka gâ'sôr nak gâ-sôr' em pü'num ai-yâ' dâk My cloth your cloth than better is	My cloth is *better* than yours.
Si ê'kum si a'la† êkum a'lem pü'num bâ-dâ-yâ' dâk This house this that house that than longer is	This house is *longer* than that.
Nâ buim pü'num â-mê-yâng' yü?* You him than younger?	Are you *younger* than he?
Men-jâk' em pü num si tâ bat-tê-ya' dâk Buffalo than elephant larger is	An elephant is *larger* than a buffalo.

3. Simple *diversity* is expressed by merely adding the comparative adjectival sign "yâ" to the positive degree of the adjective; as—

EXAMPLES.

Si	â'si	si	â-ri-yâ'	dâk	This water is *deeper*.
This	water	this	deeper	is	
A'la†	kô	a'la†	â-bui-yâ'	dâk	That child is *older*.
That	child	that	older	is	

* Interrogative of verb.

† "a'la" means *that there* person or thing in sight.

4. The superlative degree is used when the qualified noun is compared with the rest of its kind with regard to the same quality. It is formed by the insertion of "â-pui-lok'em" (the accusative of "â-pui'lok) "pü'num" = than everything, before the comparative degree; as—

EXAMPLES.

Nâ'ka	gâ'sôr		â-püi-lok'em	Your cloth is the *best of all.*
Your	cloth		all from	
	pü'num		ai-yâ' dâk	
	than		better is	
A'la*	gâ'sôr	a'la*	a-püi-lok'em	That cloth is the *finest.*
That	cloth	that	all from	
	pü'num	bâ-sôr-yâ'	dâk	
	than	finer	is	
Dû-pû-ri'ka		ken'tû	â-pui-lok'em	Dupuri's earrings are the *prettiest.*
Dupuri		earrings	all from	
pü'num		kân-kân-yâ'	dâk	
than		prettier	are	

Sî êlu sî â pui-lok em pü num bâ-dâ-yâ' mâ
This boat this all from than longer not
mui-lô a-la* êlûng ala* bâ-dâ-yâ' dû pü
If that boat that longer is possibly
— If this boat is not the *longest,* that one is.

5. The adjective is, as a rule, placed before the noun it qualifies, but it may be, and often is, placed after it without any obvious difference of meaning; as—

EXAMPLES.

Ai'na mi'ma	...	good woman.
Ai-mâ'na mi'lông	..	bad man (*lit.* not good man).
Bi-sâm'na gâ'sôr	...	thick cloth.
Û'kâ bâ-dâ'na	...	stick, long.
Ûmii bat-ti'na	...	fire, large.
Kô kân-kân'na	...	child, pretty.

6. The affix "na" is only required when the adjective is combined directly with the noun it qualifies. It is then used with it in both the comparative and the superlative degrees; as—

EXAMPLES.

Bui	â-bui-yâ'na	au'a†	He is the *elder* son.
He	elder	son	

* "a la" = demonstrative pronoun meaning *that there* person or thing (in sight).

† Nominatival "a."

Bui'ka gâ'sôr dem* pü'num His cloth it than ngôm ai-yâ'na kâ† bi'kâ. me to better give.	Give me a *better* cloth than his.
Nâ â-pui-lok'em pü'num ai-yâ'na You all from than better ê-lûng'em kâ-tô'yü ? boat seen have ?	Did you see the *best* boat ?
Ngôm â-pui-lok'em pü'num ai-yâ'na Me to all from than better gâ-sôr'kâ † bi'kâ. cloth give.	Give me the *best* boat of all.

When predicated of the noun, or used absolutely, adjectives do not need the "na," as—

EXAMPLES.

Tâ-pâm'a‡ yê-si'dâk Snow white is	Snow is white.
Si â'din si yâ'dâk This meat this rotten is	This meat is rotten.
Si gâ'sôr si bâ-sôr-yâ' dâk This cloth this thinner is	This cloth is thinner.
Gâ'lûk â-kon'a‡ yê-si' dâk â-kon'a‡ Jacket one white is one yâ-kâ' dâk black is	One jacket is white, the other black.

6.—NUMERAL ADJECTIVES.

1. The numerals from 1 to 10 are—

têr ...	1.	keng ...	6 (often abbreviated to "kî").
nyî ...	2.	kî'nit ...	7.
ûm ...	3.	pî'nyî ...	8 (4 × 2).
pî ...	4.	kâ'nâng...	9.
ngâ ...	5.	ê'ing ...	10 (often abbreviated to "ê'î").

(Miris, when counting, do not go beyond 10. After 10, they begin again at 1.)

2. To the whole of the above the suffix "kâ" (equivalent, I think, to the Assamese "tâ" in "ê'tâ" = 1, "dû-î'tâ" = 2, &c.)

---

* "dem" = demonstrative pronoun, accusative case.

† "kâ" = equivalent of English indefinite article *a*.

‡ Nominatival "a."

is added, as also a prefix "â" to the numbers from 1 to 6 inclusive; as—

EXAMPLES.

A'mî â-ûm'kâ gî-â'dâk Man three come are	Three men have (just) come.
Ngâ â'-mî kâ-nâng'kâ kâ'tô I man nine seen have	I saw nine men.

3. The numeral "one" seems to be denoted by "â'têr" (to which the suffix "kå" is regularly added), when it means *one*; but where in English the indefinite article would serve as well, the suffix "kå," with or without the prefix "â," simply is used after the noun, as—

EXAMPLES.

A'mî â-têr'kâ gî-â' dâk Man one come is	One man has (just) come.
A'mî â' kâ (*or* â-mî' kâ) gî-â 'dâk Man a come is	A man has come.
Ngôm û'kâ â-têr'kâ bî'kâ Me stick one give	Give me one stick.
Ngôm û-kâ'kâ bî'kâ Me stick a give	Give me a stick.

4. The cardinal numerals from 11 to 19 and the numerals 21 to 29, 31 to 39, &c., are formed by adding the conjunction "lâng" = *and* to the numeral "ê'ing" = 10, as—

ê'ing 'kâ lâng â-têr 'kâ =11.
ditto ditto â-nyî 'kâ =12.
&c. &c.
ê'ing â-nyî'kâ lâng â-têr'kâ=21. (lit. two tens and one.)
ditto ditto ditto â-nyî'kâ=22.
&c. &c.
ê'ing â-ûm'kâ lâng â-têr'kâ=31.
ditto ditto ditto â-nyî'kâ=32.
&c. &c.

and so on.

5. The numerals 20, 30, 40, 50, &c., to 90 are formed by adding "â-nyî'kå," "â-ûm' kå" "â-pî'kå" &c., to "ê'ing;" as—

ê'ing â-nyî'kâ=20.
do. â-ûm'kâ=30.
do. â-pî'kâ=40.
&c. &c.

6. The word for 100 is "ling," to which the suffix "kå" (alluded to in paragraph 1) is invariably added.

7. Subtraction is effected by placing the particle "nâ'pu" between the numerhend and the subtrahend, and

adding "pui mâng"=(*lit.*) *arrived not*, or, as here used, *deficient*, as—

É'î * nâ'pü â-nyî'kâ pui mâng=two less than ten.
Ê'ing â'nyî nâ'pü â-ngâ'kâ pui mâng=five less than twenty.

8. The numeral always *follows*, never *precedes*, the noun it qualifies, and is often preceded by a numerical *expletive*, or *particle*, the chief of which are—

Bâr,	to designate	rupees only.
Pîr,	„	four or two-anna pieces, pice, fowls, and birds generally.
Dôr,	„	animals.
Kông,	„	houses.
Pôm,	„	villages.
Sông,	„	long things generally, especially boats, bamboos, posts.
Muing,	„	live trees.
Bôr,	„	flat things, *i.e.*, leaves, plates, &c., also clothes.
Pui,	„	round things, *i.e.*, months (moons), eggs, kolsis, &c.

The suffix "kâ" is invariably added to the above to express *one*, and the numerals "nyî," "ûm," "pî," "ngâ," "keng," or "ê'ing," with or without the suffix "kâ," to express the numbers 2, 3, 4, 5, 6, or 10.

These numeral particles are *never* used with the numerals 7, 8, or 9.

EXAMPLES.

(*Illustrating use of numerical particles.*)

Say eggs are being counted—

Â'pui pui'kâ= 1 egg.
pui'nyî= 2 eggs.
pui'ûm= 3 „
pui'pî= 4 „
pui'ngâ= 5 „
pui'keng= 6 „
kî'nit= 7 „
pî'nyî= 8 „
kâ'nâng= 9 „
pui ê'ing=10 „

"Á'pui" having been *once* mentioned is sufficient to show that the enumeration refers to eggs, and hence no repetition of the noun is required.

As the final "ng" (*vide* note opposite consonant *n*) in the numerical particles "kông," "sông," "muing," is dropped with

* "nâ'pu"=Assam "hô-bô-lû'î" *i.e.*, *to be*, so that "ê'î nâ'pü"=ten to be.

certain numerals, it may be as well to exemplify these particles in their abbreviated form:—

È'kum'kông'kâ=1house	Ê'lûng sông'kâ=1boat	Ur'sing â-muing'kâ =1tree.
kô'nyî =2 „	sô'nyi =2 „	mui nyî=2 „
kông'ûm =3 „	sông'um =3 „	muing'ûm=3 „
kô'pî =4 „	sô'pî =4 „	mui'pî =4 „
kô'ngâ =5 „	sô'ngâ =5 „	mui'ngâ =5 „
kông'keng=6 „	sông'keng=6 „	muing'keng=6 „
kî'nit =7 „	kî'nit =7 „	ditto =7 „
pî'nyî =8 „	pî'nyî =8 „	ditto =8 „
kâ'nâng =9 „	kâ'nâng =9 „	ditto =9 „
kô ê'ing=10 „	sô ê'ing =10 „	mui ê'ing=10 „

Further Examples.

(Illustrating manner of using numerical particles in conversation.)

Ngôm mûr'kông bâr-pî'kâ bî'kâ Me rupee four give	Give me Rs. 4.
Ngâ buim mûr'kông bâr-ngâ'kâ bî'tô I him rupee five given have	I gave him Rs. 8.
Ngôm po'rok pîr-pî'kâ bî'kâ Me fowl four give	Give me four fowls.
Bui po'rok pîr-keng'kâ mô-kê'tô He fowls six killed has	He killed six fowls.
Ngâ shî'râ dôr-nyî'kâ âp'tô I pig (wild) two shot have	I shot two wild pigs.
Bui sî'mon dôr-ûm'kâ kâ'tô He deer three seen has	He saw three deer.
Ngâ'ka ur' sâ dôr-nyi'kâ ê'ek kî-nit'kâ dûng My "mithon" two pig seven are	I have two "mithon" and seven pigs.
Sî dâ'lû sî kô-ngâ'kâ dûng This village this house five are	This village has five houses.
Nâ'ka dâ'lûng kô'ê-ing-â"* kâ dûng Your village house ten only are.	Your village has only ten houses.
Sî ô'pê sî pôm pî'kâ dûng This tribe this village four are	This tribe has four villages.
Â'mî â'lâk sô-nyî'kâ â'mik â-nyî'kâ dûng Man arm two eyes two are	A man has two arms and two eyes.
Bui sin'ying ê'lûng sô-ngâ'ka pâ'tô He this year boat five cut has	He cut five boats this year.
Ngâ'kâ â'bûk sông-keng'kâ dûng My gun six are	I have six guns.
Gâ'rû â'lê sô-pî'kâ dûng	... The cow has four legs.
Buim gâ'sôr bôr-ûm'kâ bî'to-kâ Him cloth three give	Give him three cloths.

* "â"=particle, meaning *only*.

Bui ur'sing* â'muing muing-ûm'kâ tê'tô. He tree three cut has.	He cut down three trees.
Kô'pâk ê'kâm† bôr ê-ing'kâ nât- Plantain leaf ten cut bôm'kû"kâ. bring.	Cut and bring ten plantain-leaves.
Ngôm â'pui pui-ngâ'kâ bi'kâ. Me egg five give.	Give me five eggs.

9. Certain words—though not very many, for I can only remember those given—in *combination* with *numerals* lose their *first* syllables; as—

EXAMPLES.

Dû'tâk = a year.
- tâng-nyî'kâ = 2 years.
- tâng-ûm'kâ = 3 „
- tâk-pî'kâ = 4 „
- tâ-ngâ'kâ = 5 „
- tâ-keng'kâ = 6 „
- dû'tâk kî-nit'kâ = 7 „
- &c., &c.

Bôm'yâm = fathom.
- yâm'kâ = 1 fathom.
- yâm-ngâ'kâ = 5 „
- bôm'yâm ê-ing'kâ = 10 „
- &c., &c.

Lâg'dû = cubit.
- dû'kâ = 1 cubit.
- dû-nyî'kâ = 2 „
- dû-ngâ'kâ = 5 „
- &c., &c.

Pin'gop = span.
- gop'kâ = 1 span.
- gop-nyî'kâ = 2 „
- gop-ûm'kâ = 3 „
- &c., &c.

Â'pui = egg.
- â-pui'kâ = 1 egg.
- pui'nyî = 2 „
- pui'ngâ = 3 „
- &c., &c.

Ur'sing â'muing = tree.
- ur'sing â-muing'kâ = 1 tree.
- mui-nyî'kâ = 2 „
- mui-ûm'kâ = 3 „
- muing-keng'kâ = 6 „
- &c., &c.

---

* "ur'sing" = wood generally, "ur'sing â'muing" = a (live) tree.

† "ê'kâm" = any large leaf which could be used for eating rice off: other leaves are called "ur'sing â'na."

The following examples will illustrate how these words in their abbreviated form are used in conversation :—

Ngâ Kâ-lî-kâ'tâ ba'lâ tâng-nyî'kâ dûng'ai I Calcutta there years two was	I was two years in Calcutta.
Bui ur'sing mui-ê-ing'kâ tê'tô He tree ten fell has	He has felled ten trees.
Sî ê'lû sì yâm-pî'kâ bâ-dâ'dûng This boat this fathom four long is	This boat is four fathoms long.
* Ngôm dû-ngâ'na† gâ-sòr'kâ bî'kâ Me cubit five cloth a give	Give me a five cubit cloth.
Da û'ka da gop-é-ing'kâ dûng That stick that span ten is	That stick is ten spans.

10. The adverbial numerals are formed by prefixing "lê" to the numerals, to which latter the suffix "kâ" is also regularly added ; as—

Lê-têr'kâ ... once.
Lê-nyî'kâ ... twice.
Lê-ûm'ka ... thrice.
&c., &c.

Ordinals.

There are no ordinals in Miri. The particle "pô" = *foremost in time*, or *place*, answers to our English ordinal of one (*first*), while "mê-lâm'pü" = *subsequently*, or "da-lok'ka" = *afterwards* (*lit.* "da" = *that*, "lok" = *from*, with the euphonic "ka" noticed *ante*) is used in lieu of the remaining ordinals (*second*, *third*, &c., &c.); as—

Examples.

Ngâ'ka âp-pô-dâ dem ‡ ai-tô mâ ngâ'ka My shooting first whilst good has not my mê-lâm'pü âb-dâ § dem ai-dûng'ai subsequently shooting whilst good was.	My first shot was bad, my second a good one.

* This sentence might be equally correctly made by placing the noun first; as—
"Ngôm gâ-sor dû-ngâ'na kâ bî'kâ."

† Adjectival "na."

‡ âp-dâ'dem = adverbial participle of root verb "âp" = shoot.

§ The "p" is changed into a "b" for sake of euphony.

Ma'lô ngâ sî-mon'em lem * -ngâ'kâ Yesterday I deer five times âp'tô sî-mon'a † mô-tî'lâ dâg'ai shoot have deer far (place) in stood, or was Ngâ'ka âp-pô-dâ' dem ai-tô'mâ My shooting first whilst good has not (been) mê-lâm'pü âb-dâ' dem ai-gâm'kâng afterwards shooting whilst good little became da-lok'ka râ-dâng'ka âb'nâm da‡ that from (after that) middle of shot it bek'tô bek-dâk'kôm ai'pü bek'mâng. bit has hitting well hit not. Da lô sî-mon a † ân-jâ ka dûk-dûng'ai Then deer little running was dûk-dâ'dem ê'gü lô-nyi'ka âp-tem-tô'kü § running whilst again twice fire have bek'mâng hit not	Yesterday I had five shots at a deer which was a long way off. My first shot was not a good one, but the second was better, and at the third shot I hit it, but not hard. The deer then moved off, and I had a fourth and fifth shot at it, but missed.
Ngâ'ka gî-dâ-lông-a' † dem ‡ Nâp'shû My going day Nap shu dâ-lû' lâ pui' tô da ‡ ka mê'lâm village to arrived have that of next lông-a'lâ pô'dông ô'kâ da-lok'ka lô-nyi' lâ day on rain fell that from days two on tê pô'dông ô'ka also rain fell	On the first day I reached Napshú village, and on the second day it rained, on the third and fourth days it also rained.

III.—Pronouns.

1. Miri pronouns are of four kinds, *viz.*, personal, relative, interrogative, and adjective.

7.—Personal Pronouns.

Singular.

Nom.	Ngâ ... I.	Nâ............ thou.	Bui ...... he, or she.
Acct. & Dat.	Ngôm...me, to me.	Nom ......you, to you.	Buim ... his or her to ditto.
Poss.	Ngâ'ka, of me.	Nâ'ka ......of you.	Bui' ka...of his, her.
‖	Ngâ'kem mine.	‖ Nâ' kem ... yours.	‖ Bui'ken... his, hers.
Abl.	Ngâ-ka' lok. from me.	Nâ-ka'lok... from you.	Bui-ka'lok, from his, hers.

* Adverbial numeral prefix, with "m" attached for sake of euphony.

† Nominatival "a."

‡ Demonstrative pronoun.

§ "Kû"=affirmative participle.

‖ Pronominal adjectives equivalent to "môr" in Assamese.

Plural.

Nom.	Ngâ' lû... we.	Nâ'lû......... you.	Bû'lû ...... they.
Act. & Dat.	Ngâ' lûm, us, to us.	Nâ'lûm ...... you, to you.	Bû'lûm ... them, to them.
Poss.	Ngâ-lû'ka, of us.	Nâlû' ka ... of you.	Bû-lû' ka.. of them.
	* Ngâ-lû'kem, ours.	* Nâ-lû' kem... yours.	* Bû-lû' kem theirs.
Abl.	Ngâ-lû-ka' lok. from us.	Nâ-lû-ka'lok from you.	Bû-lu-ka'lok from them.

N.B.—There being no passive voice in Miri, the case of the agent cannot be expressed.

2. For the plural of these (personal) pronouns â-puing =*all* is used ; as—

EXAMPLES.

Â-pông' em nâ' lûm â-puing' em. Liquor you to all kê' bâng'† em ngâ bî' tô council I given have.	I gave the liquor to you all.
Â-lô' em nâ or-bî‡ yô-ka bû' lû Salt you distribute not they â-puing' a§ or-shû-ye pü all distribute will	Don't you distribute the salt; they will themselves distribute it.

N.B.—The *repetition* of the third person singular personal pronoun after the noun is a noteable feature of the Miri language ; as—

EXAMPLES.

Dû'mai bui da'pü lû'tô Dumai he thus spoken has.	Dumai said so (*i.e.*, thus spoke).
Dû-pû'rî bui ai'rûp lä-bâg dûk Dupuri she very lazy is	Dupuri is very lazy.
Dû'mai bui mû' jî mâ Dumai he old not	Dumai is not old.

3. The reflective pronoun is "aî'yü," and is thus declined ; as—

SINGULAR AND PLURAL.

Nom.	Aî'yü	self, selves.
Acct. & Dat.	Aî'yûm	self, selves, to ditto.
Poss.	Aî'ka	of self, own.
Abl.	Aî-ka'lok..............	from self, selves.

* Pronominal adjectives equivalent to "mor" in Assamese.

† kê' bâng (village) assembly; here, however, kê bâng means "collectively," nâ 'lûm â-puing'em=you all, kê bâng em=collectively.

‡ "or-bî" two root verbs ("or"=distribute, "bî"=give) compounded together.

§ Nominatival "a."

EXAMPLES.

Bui ai'yü mô-kê-shû'* to He self kill has	He killed himself.
Ngôm ai'yûm bi'kâ Me to self give	Give it to me myself.
Sî bû-lû'ka ai'ka This their own	This is their own.
Sî gâ'sôr sî nâ'ka ai-ka'yü?† This cloth this your own?	Is this cloth your own?

4. There is no *neuter* pronoun, answering to the English third person neuter pronoun *it*, in Miri. It is, however, a common practice to use the demonstrative pronoun "da" after the noun for emphasis; as—

EXAMPLES.

Nâ'ka gâ'sôr da koi-â' dâk Your cloth it dirty is	Your cloth is dirty.
Gá'sôr dem ngôm bi'kâ Cloth it me to give	Give me the cloth.

8.—RELATIVE PRONOUNS.

1. There are no relative pronouns in Miri equivalent to the English *who*, *what*, *which*, or the Bengali যিনি (*who*) যে (*what*, *which*).

Their place is generally supplied by a *participle*. As, however, the construction of relative clauses is a highly idiomatic business, it will be as well to exemplify it somewhat fully by illustrations:—

EXAMPLES.

Ngâ'ka ma-lô'ka kâ'nâm‡ My yesterday seen â'mî da§ sî da kû man he this (man) verily	This is the man *whom* I saw yesterday (*i.e.*, this is the man seen of me).
Ngâ'ka mûr'kông â-bâr'kâ bi'nâm‖ My rupee one given â'mî da man he	The man *to whom* I gave a rupee.

---

* "shû" is a reflective verbal particle.

† Interrogative of verb.

‡ "kâ'nâm"=participle past passive of root verb "kâ"=see.

§ "da" and "sî da"=demonstrative pronouns.

‖ "bi'nam"=past participle passive of root verb "bi"=give.

Ngâ'ka â'buk lâ'nâm* â'mî da My gun taken man he	The man *from whom* I took a gun.
Me lam ka gla na ami da a pui lok em pu nam ai ya dak	The man who came last is the best.
Ma-yum'ka ü'mü ûg'nâm* Yesterday evening fire caught ê'kum da yâ'lâ ô-lek'kâng house it night in fell	The house *that* was burnt last evening fell in the night.
Ngâ'ka bôm'yâm yâm-kî'nâm* My fathom measured ê'lû da boat it	The boat *which* I measured.
Gô rû† sî na‡ da-lok'ka Cow dead that from of rû tûm'a owner.	The man *whose* cow died.
Ngôm sim gâ'sôr sim bî'na‡ â'mî Me to this cloth this giver man da sî kâng he dead	The man *who* gave this cloth is dead.
Ma-lo'ka shâ'ben kî'na‡ da Yesterday goat sick it sî'lô ai-kâng'kû this day well became	The goat *that* was ill yesterday has recovered to-day.

2. In the last two illustrations given above the relative clause is turned, by the help of the participle, into an *adjectival clause*, which qualifies the noun that in a proper relative clause would be the *subject* of the relative. This noun thus qualified being reinforced by the addition of the redundant "da," which recalls attention to the true subject of the sentence. This is a very common mode of turning a relative clause in Miri.

3. Sometimes two simple predications are made to turn a relative clause; as—

EXAMPLES.

Â-mî'kâ§ kâ-tû'ai sî da kû‖ Man a saw this he verily	This is the man *whom* I saw (I saw a man. This is he verily).
Bui sî-mon'kâ§ âp-tû'ai sî da‖ He deer a shot this it kû verily	This is the deer *which* he shot. (He shot a deer. This is it.)

* "lâ'nâm"=past participle passive of "lâ"=take; "ûg'nâm"=ditto of "ûk"=burn; "yâm-kî'nâm"=ditto of "yâm'kî"=fathom, measure.

† "Gô'rû"=Assam. Miris have no word.

‡ Adjectival "na".

§ "kâ" is equivalent to our English indefinite article *a*.

‖ "sî da"=demonstrative pronoun.

4. Relative clauses may likewise be turned by using the demonstrative pronoun "da" *doubled* in conjunction with "dâk'kôm," the present participle of the verb *to be*, and when so used "da da dâk'kôm" (lit. *that, that, being*) appears to have the *force* and *meaning* of the relative pronoun *whatever*; as—

EXAMPLES.

Da da dâk'kôm bâzârâ ai' na* That that being bázár in good pö'rók dû di † lâ-tô-i'kâ. ‡ fowls be may bring.	Bring from the bázár *what* good fowls there may be.
Da da â mi dák kôm ngôm Mi shing That that man being me Miri â-gôm em lû-yir-yê'mui"lô buim mûr'kông language teach will if him to rupee bi'pü. give will.	I will reward the man *who* teaches me Miri.

5. "In'qua in'qua dû'di" = lit. *what, what, be will*, is also used to turn a relative clause; as—

EXAMPLES.

Nâ ka ê-gin'lâ in'qua in'qua dû 'di† Your basket in what what be may ngôm bi'kâ me to give	Give me *what* you have in your basket.
Nâ ka dâ-lû'lâ in'qua in'qua mi'ûm mûk'shâ Your village in what what girls shâ'na dû'di† ngôm len-kân-lângkâ. be may me to show.	Show me what dancing girls you have in your village.

RELATIVE CLAUSES OF *time*, *place*, AND *manner*.

6. The following examples will illustrate how these are turned in Miri:—

EXAMPLES.

Nâ ta'lâ§ gi-yê-mui'lô buim gi-lâng'kâ You there go will if him to go em'to-kâ. say	*When* you go there, tell him to come.

---

* Adjectival "na."

† "di" = particle of vague probability.

‡ "lâ-tô-i'ka = Assamese "â-ni'â di'bi = fetch!

§ "ta'lâ" = a place up stream, "ba'lâ = a place down stream.

Nâ'ka dâ-lûng'a * in-kâ'lâ dû'na ?† Your village (*lit.*) what in is? *i.e.*, where ngôm len-kân-yî'kâ. me to show.	Show me *where* your village is.
A-dî-lô'dî ‡ ngâ sî-mon'em kâ-yê-'mui"lô Whenever I deer see will if âp'dâ. I shoot.	*Whenever* I see a deer I shoot it.
Pô'dông ô-yê-'mui"lô tâ-pât'a* len'dâ Rain fall will if leeches come out	*When* it rains, the leeches come out.
Da'lâ da'lâ dâkkôm â'sî pâ-yê'pü. There there going water find will.	(You) will find water wherever (you go).
Da'pü da'pü î-dûk'kôm ai-pü-lâng'â.§ That wise that wise doing will not.	However you do it, it will not be good.

9.—Interrogative Pronouns.

"Sê'kô" = *who?* It is thus declined:—

Singular and Plural.

Nom.	Sê'kô	who?
Acct. } Dat. }	Sê'kom ...	whom? to whom?
Poss.	Se'ka	of whom?
Abl.	Se-ka'lok...	from whom?

Examples.

Illustrating how used.

Nôm sê'kô pâ-tô'na ?† You who struck?	Who struck you?
Nâ sê'kôm kâ-tô'na ?† You whom seen have?	Whom did you see?
Nâ se'ka â-gôm'em lû-dû'na ?† You whose word speaking are?	Of whom are you speaking?
Bui se-ka'lok pâ-tô'na? He who from received have?	From whom did he get it?

"In'kâ?" or "in qua?" = *what? which?* thus declined:—

Singular and Plural.

Nom.	In'kâ *or* in'qua?......	what? which?
Acct. }	In'kôm *or* in'quom?.	what?
Dat. }	In-kâ'lôm?............	which?
Poss.	In-kâ'kâ?	of what? which?
Abl.	In-kâ'lok?	from what? which?
Loc.	In-kâ'lâ?...............	in what, which? (where?)

---

* Nominatival "a."
† Interrogative of verb.
‡ "di" = particle of vague probability.
§ Negative interrogative.

EXAMPLES.

Illustrating how used.

Si in'qua na ?* This what ?	What is this ?
Nâ in'kôm î-dû'na ?* You what doing ?	What are you doing ?
Bui nâ'ka (*or* nâ-ka'pü) in-qua'na ?* He your what ?	What (relation) is he to you ?
Nâ in'kôm em-dû'na ?* You what saying ?	What are you saying ?
Bui in-kâ'kâ lû-dû'na ?* He what of saying ?	What is he saying ? (of what is he speaking ?)
Sim in-kâ'lok mô-dû'na ?* This what from made is ?	What is this made of ?
Nâ in-kâ'lâ ma-tô'na ?* You what in put have ?	Where (in what) have you put it ?
Ngâ in'ka lâm-bü'lok gî-yê'na ?* I which road by go shall ?	Which road shall I go by ?
Nâ in-ka'lôm lâ-yê'na ?* You which take will ?	Which will you take ?

"Ka'pi" (which is *indeclinable*) is used apparently as an adjective pronoun in the sense of *what sort, what kind, what matter, in what manner,* &c., as—

EXAMPLES.

Ngâ kâ-pî'na† gâ'sôr rê-yê'na ?* I what sort cloth buy shall ?	What sort of cloth shall I buy ?
Bui kâ-pi'na a mi a ?	...What kind of person is he ?
Ngâ'ka gâ-sôr'em pot-shû'tô. My cloth torn have. Kâ-pi'kân ?* What matter ?	I have torn my cloth. What matter ?
Nâ'ka â'mik da‡ kâ-pi-kâ'na ?* Your eyes they what matter ?	What is the matter with your eyes ?

"A-dit'kâ" =*how much? how many?* not declined :—

EXAMPLES.

Illustrating how used.

Sâk'ka§ nâ'ka dâ-lûng'a ‖ a-dit'kâ This from your village how much mô-tî-yâ'¶ dû'na ?* farther is ?	How much farther is your village from this ?

---

* Interrogative of verb.
† Adjectival "na."
‡ Demonstrative pronoun.
§ "sâk" =*this from* "ka" euphonic.
‖ Nominatival "a."
¶ Comparative adjectival sign.

Nâ pô-lô'lâ a-dit'kâ âm-bnin'-em You month in how much rice dâ-lâ-pui'â ?* eat able will?	How much rice can you eat in a month ?
Nâ sî-mon'em a-dit'kâ kâ-to'na?* You deer how many seen have?	How many deer did you see?
Nâ'ka dâ-lû'lâ mî-long'a† a-dit'kâ Your village in men how many dû'na ?* are?	How many men are there in your village?

"A-dî'lô ?" = *when?* "A-dî-lok'ka?" = *when, from* (from what time ?)

Examples.

Illustrating how used.

Ngâ a-dî'lô nôm kâng-kâ'pü I when you see purpose of gî-â-yê'na ? come shall?	When shall I come to see you?
Nâ'lû a-dî'lô gi-lâ‡-yê-kû'na? You when return will?	When will you return (home)?
Sim gâ'sôr sim a-dî-lok'ka This cloth this when from shûm-dû'na ? wearing are?	Since when are you wearing this cloth?

Adjective Pronouns.

Adjective pronouns are of three kinds, *viz.*, possessive, demonstrative, and indefinite.

Possessive.

The place of a regular possessive pronoun is supplied by the *possessive case* of the *personal* pronouns; as—

Examples.

Si gâ'sor sî ngâ'ka. This cloth this mine.	This cloth is mine.
Sî ê'gin sî nga-lû-ka'yü ?* This basket this ours?	Is this basket ours?

My father, mother, sister, &c., &c., are formed by simply placing the word father, or mother, &c., after the genitive case

---

* Interrogative of verb.

† Nominatival "a."

‡ This "lâ" is short for "lât"—"gi-lât'to-kâ" = *return*; "kû" is the affirmative particle.

of the pronoun, and adding the third person singular personal pronoun "bui," as—

EXAMPLES.

Ngá'ka bâ'bû bui. My father he.	My father.
Ngá' ka bâ-bû bui mû-jing-kâ'vong.* My father he old is.	My father is old.
Bui'ka pai bui sí'kâng. His uncle he dead.	His uncle is dead.

If the plural termination of the noun be used, the personal pronoun after it is not required; as—

EXAMPLE.

Bui'ka buir'ma kî-ding'a† kân-kan'-dâk. His sisters pretty are.	His sisters are pretty.

10.—DEMONSTRATIVE PRONOUNS.

The *demonstrative pronouns* are—

Sî=*this* person, or thing, *near.*	Da=*that* person, or thing, *near.*
Sî da= ditto (more emphatic).	A da= ditto (more emphatic).

A la=*that* person or thing *there, in sight,* but a little way off.

"Si" is thus declined:—

Singular and Plural.

Nom.	Sî	this person, or thing.
Acct. & Dat.	Sim	this person, or thing, to ditto.
Poss.	Sâ'ka ...	of this person, or thing.
Abl.	Sâk	from this person, or thing.

"Da" is similarly declined, but it has also the loc. case [da'lâ (in that there)]. "It is in this" would be—

Sî â'râ sî dûng
This inside this is.

"Sî da," and "a da," appear to have the nominative, accusative, and dative cases only. For the latter two "em" is tacked on to the "d" instead of "a," making "sî dem," "a dem," respectively.

"A la" is declined like "sî."

---

* "kâ'vô"—"kâ" is the tense suffix, with "vô," the intensive completive particle, attached to it.

† Nominatival "a."

N.B.—"Sî da" and "a da" when standing alone as a predicate require to be strengthened by the affirmative particle "kû;" as—

Examples.

Ngâ â-mî'kâ* kâ-tû'ai sî da kû. I man saw, this he verily.	This is the *very* man I saw (I saw a man, this is he *verily*).
Bui ê-lûng'kâ* pâ-tû'ai a da kû. He boat cut, this it verily.	That is the *very* boat he cut.

The ***repetition*** of the demonstrative pronouns after the noun is a noticeable feature of the language.

Examples.

Illustrating how demonstrative pronouns are used.

Sî mî'ma sî Dû-mai'ka This woman this Dumai' me-ang'a†. wife.	This woman is Dumai's wife.
Sim gâ'sôr sim ngâ kâ'pü î-yê'na?‡ This cloth this I what do shall?	What shall I do with this cloth?
Sî men'jâk sî sâ ka â'mî This buffalo this this of man sâ-ka'yü?‡ this of?	Is this buffalo this man's?
Nâ sâk â'mî sâk pâ-tô'- You this from man this from get yü?‡ have?	Did you get it from this man?
Sâk gâ'sôr kî'dî sâk â-sî'a† This from cloths these from water len'dâk. coming out is.	Water is dripping from these cloths.
Da â'mî da rû-bê'dâk. That man that deaf is	That man is deaf.
Dem â'mî kî'dî dem gî-gê-mô'tokâ.§ Those men those send away.	Send those men away.
Dak â'mî dak gâ-sôr'em That from man that from cloth pâ'tô nâ kâ-pî'lâ lû-mâ'- received have you why say na?‡ not?	Why didn't you say you got the cloth from that man.

---

* "kâ" equivalent to English indefinite article "a."

† Nominatival "a."

‡ Interrogative of verb.

§ Compound verb "gi"=go, "gê"=scold, with causal "mô" added.

Dak'ka mê'lâm da That from of (man) next he sê-kô'na?* who?	Who is the next man?
Da gâ'sôr da da'ka â'mî da-ka'- That cloth that that of man that yü?* of?	Is that cloth that man's?
Da'lâ in'qua du'na?* That in what is?	What is in that?
Sî da â'mî sî da ngôm pâ'tô. This very man this me struck.	This very man struck me.
Sî dem a'mî kî'dî sî dem ngâ These very men these I kâng-kü'mâ. saw never.	I never saw these men.
A da â'mî a da ngôm tû'tô. That very man that me kicked.	That very man kicked me.
Adem â'mî kî'dî dem ngâ Those very men those I bî-to'mâ. gave not.	I did not give to those men.
A la gâ'lûk a la ân-jâ'dâk. That there jacket that small is.	That (there) jacket is small.
A la â'mî a la â-nû'pü That there man that newly gî-â'na.† comer.	That man there is a new comer.
A la ur'sing â-muing'a‡ a la That there tree that lün'ying ai-ê-yê'pü. next year fruit will.	That tree there will bear fruit next year.

11.—INDEFINITE PRONOUNS.

Those most commonly used are—

Sê-kô'dî‡=somebody (lit., whoever, *i.e.*, sê'kô=who? dî, particle of vague probability).
Mûm'kâ=somebody (lit., strange one).
Sê-kô'tê (or sin) kâ mâ=nobody (lit., who even exists not).
Â-tî-kô'tê (sin) kâ mâ=nothing.
Â'kon=some.
Â'kâ‡=ditto.
Ân-jâ-kâ‡'tê=some more (lit., little also).
Lê-kô'tê=some more (lit., again also).
Bâ-jê'kâ§=many, much.

---

* Interrogative of verb.
† Adjectival "na."
‡ Nominatival "a."
§ The same "kâ" as is found attached to numerals.

No word for examples showing how English sentences containing same are turned.	=as many as.
Ditto ditto *vide* page 70=all.	
Ditto ditto ditto =each.	

EXAMPLES.

Illustrating how indefinite pronouns are used.

Sê-kô'dî nî-tôm'a mô'dûng. Some one singing is.	*Someone* is singing.
Sê-kô'dî gî-âng-kâ'yü? Some one come has?	Has *anyone* come?
Sim gû'sôr sim sê-kô'dî mô-pet'tô. This cloth this some one torn has.	*Someone* has torn this cloth.
Sê-kô'dî gi-â'dâk. Some one come has.	*Someone* has (just) come.

The use of "sê-kô'dî" appears to be restricted to cases such as those given above, while the particle "mûm," to which the numeral suffix "kâ" is attached, appears to be very *generally* used, either for *persons* or *things*, as—

EXAMPLES.

Â'mî mûm'kâ gî-â-dâk. A person come has.	*Someone* has come.
Â'mî mûm'kâ gôk-tô-kâ'kâ. A person call.	Call *someone*.
Ngâ in'kôm â-mî'em gôg'yen?* I whom man call shall?	Whom shall I call?
Da da dâk'kom â'mî mûm'kâ gôk'to-kâ. That that being a person call.	*Anyone*, call *someone*.
Bâ-zâr'lok gâ'sôr mûm'kâ bôm-â-lâng'kâ Bazar from cloth any one bring.	Bring *some* cloth from the bazar.
Ê-kum'lâ sê'kô dû'na?† House in who is?	Who is in the house?
Sê-kô-tê kâ mâ (*or* â'mî kâ mâ) Any one at all exists not man exists not.	*Nobody*.
Ngâ sê-kôm-a'tê bi-gê'mâ. I anyone at all give will not.	I will give it to *nobody*.
Ngâ'lû sê-kôm-a'tê ken'mûng. We any one at all know not.	*None of us* can tell.

---

* This is a mere abbreviation of the future tense suffix "yê" and the interrogative "na."

† Interrogative of verb.

Ngâ â-ti-kô'sin lû'mâ. I anything at all say not.	I did not say *anything.*
Ngâ â-ti-kô'tê kô'mâ. I anything at all seek not.	I wish for *nothing.*
Î-pô'num* â-ti-kô'sin kâ-mû'- Do first anything at all exists vông. no more.	There is *nothing* more to be done.
Ê-ek'a† â'kon â'kon jü'dâ Pigs some fat â'kon â'kon shâ'dâ. some lean.	*Some* pigs are fat, *some* lean.
Â'kâ‡ â'kâ kô'a† â-gin'pü Some children always kâp-ti'dâ. crying continuously are.	*Some* children are always crying.
Ân-jâ-kâ'tê ngôm bi'kâ. Little also me to give.	Give me some *more.*
Ngôm bâ-jê'kâ bi'kâ. Me to much (or many) give.	Give me *much,* or *many.*

The following examples will illustrate how English sentences containing, "*as much as,*" "*as many as,*" are turned in Miri:—

EXAMPLES.

Nâ a-dit'kâ dâ'pü dâ-lâ-dâ'na You how much eat to eat able are dâ-lâng'kâ. eat.	Eat *as much as* you can.
Si'lô kê'sha yâm-pô tê dâ-rê'- This day like morrow also sun- mui"lô âm'a† min-yê'pü. shine if "dhan" ripen will.	If (we have) *as much* sunshine to-morrow *as* (we had) to-day the "dhan" will ripen.
Nâ'ka mûr'kông a-dit'kâ dû'na§ Your rupees how many are ngôm â-pui'dem bi'kâ. me to whole give.	Give me *as many* rupees *as* you have.
Nâ mûr'kông a-dit'kâ lâ-lâ-dâ'- You rupees how many take able na nâ'ka â-lâk'lâ pui-nâm'kô are your hand in filled lâ-tô-lâng'kâ. take (away).	Take *as many* rupees *as* your hand (will) hold.

---

* "pô" particle of priority.

† Nominatival "a."

‡ "Â'kon" *or* "Â'kâ" may be placed either before, or after the noun.

§ Interrogative of verb.

Nâ a-dit'kâ â-mî'em pâ-dâ'na You how many men get yâm'pô gî-vô†-lâng'kâ. morrow bring with (you).	Bring* *as many* men *as* you (can) get to-morrow.

All is expressed by the particle "in," or "âm," which are placed *between* the root and the tense suffix; as—

EXAMPLES.

Men-jâk'a‡ Buffaloes	sî-in'kâng. all died *or* sî-âm'kang.	*All* the buffaloes died.
Ê-ek'tê sî-in-yë'pü. Pigs also die all will.		(The) pigs also will *all* die.

The following illustrations will show how English sentences containing *each* are turned in Miri:—

EXAMPLES.

Â'mî â-mi â âm-buin'em pâ-tô'- Man man to rice received mui'lô da-lok'ka§ bû'lû in'kôm if that from they what kô-dû'na? require?	If *each* man has received rice, what more do they want?
Â'mî â'mî â'gêr gêr-nâm‖'em âng'ü Man man working separate âng-ü'pü ngôm len-kân-yî'kâ. separately me to show.	Show me *each* man's work separately.
Nâ'lûm lê'têr lê-têr'kâ âb-mô'pü. You once once fire permit will.	I will let you *each* fire a shot.
Sim â'mî kî'dî sim â'-mî â'-mî'kâ These men these man man â'bâr¶ â-bâr'kâ bi'tô-kâ. one rupee one rupee give.	Give *each* of these men one rupee.

12.—IV.—VERBS.

The Miri verb, like the Kachari one, "is," to quote from the Revd. Mr. Endle's Kachari Grammar, page 16, the most "difficult part of the language to deal with," and for the same reasons too, *viz.*, "not so much from its structure, or conjugation, which is perfectly regular, as from the fact that the usage

---

* Interrogative of verb.

† "vô," permissive particle signifies here "a bringing *with.*"

‡ Nominatival "a."

§ Demonstrative pronoun, abl. case.

‖ "Gêr'nâm"=past participle of root verb "â'gêr,"=work, with accusative case suffix, used here as a verbal noun.

¶ "bâr" is a numeral particle used to designate rupees, *vide* page 40 *ante*.

and exact force of the different tenses is uncertain, some of these, especially those expressive of *past* time, being apparently sometimes used interchangeably." Again the Miri verb also "admits of being compounded, not only with other verbal roots, but with adjectives, adverbs, and various affixes which serve materially to modify its meaning."

As in Kachari every Miri verb is conjugated from a verbal root, or stem (the roots only of verbs have been given in the vocabulary at the end of this work) and the different relations of tense, mood, &c., are expressed by suffixes attached directly to the verbal root, an additional letter being occasionally inserted between the root and the suffix expressive of time (or a letter is occasionally changed)to prevent a disagreeable hiatus.

SUBSTANTIVE VERB.

There are *two* forms of this verb, *viz.*, "dûng," and "dak," but they have only the present, and past tenses; as—

PRESENT TENSE.

Singular.	*Plural.*
Ngâ dûng *or* dâk... I am.	Ngâ'lû dûng *or* dâk ... we are.
Nâ dûng „ dâk ... thou art.	Nâlû dung „ dâk ... you are.
Bui dûng „ dâk ... he, or she, is.	Bû'lû dûng „ dâk ... they are.

PAST TENSE.

Singular.	*Plural.*
Ngâ dûng'ai *or* dâg'ai ... I was.	Ngâ'lû dûng'ai *or* dâg'ai. we were.
Nâ dûng'ai „ dâg'ai ... thou wert.	Nâ'lû dûng'ai „ dâg'ai. you were.
Bui dûng'ai „ dâg'ai ... he, or she, was.	Bû'lû dûngai „ dâg'ai. they were.

Negation with these verbs is formed by substituting "kâ mâ," or "kâ mâng,"=*exists not*, for "dûng," "dâk," and "kâ mâng'ai" for "dûng'ai," "dâg'ai"; as—

EXAMPLES.

Bui sâ dûng. He here is.	He is here.
Bui sâ kâ mâ. He here not.	He is not here.
Â'sî* â-bû'lâ ê'ngâ dûng. River in fish are.	There are fish in the river.
Â'sî â-bû'lâ ê'ngâ kâmâng. River in fish none.	There are no fish in the river.
Bui sâ dûng'ai. He here was.	He was here.

* â'si â'bûng=abounding with water, â'bû=whole, entire.

Bui sâ kâ mâng'ai. **He here not was.**	He was not here.
Â'sî â-bû'lâ ê'ngâ dûng'ai. **River in fish were.**	There were fish in the river.
Â'sî â-bû'lâ ê'ngâ kâ mâng'ai. **River in fish not were.**	There were no fish in the river.
Ngâ'ka â-lâk'lâ â-tî-kô'tê kâ mâ. **My hand in anything at all exists not.**	There is nothing in my hand.
Ngâ'ka â-lâk'lâ a-tî-kô'sin. kâ mâng'ai. **My hand in any thing at all existed not.**	There was nothing in my hand.
Sî dâ'lû sî ki'na* dû'yü† ? **This village this sick are?**	Are there any sick (people) in this village ?
Kî'na* kâ mâ. **Sick none.**	There are none.
Kâ mâ mui'lô rê-tô-kâ'kâ.‡ **Exists not if buy go (bring).**	If there is none go buy (and bring).

"Dûng" is apparently used to indicate what is *definitely* going on at some point of *present* time; as—

EXAMPLES.

Bui sâ dûng. **He here is.**	He is (*now*) here.
Ngâ kî dûng. **I ill is.**	I am (*just now*) ill.
Ngâ ai'dûng. **I well is.**	I am (*at present*) well.
Bui â-pin'em dâ'dûng. **He rice eating is.**	He is (*now*) eating rice.
Ê-kî'a§ râ'dûng. **Dog barking is.**	The dog is (*now*) barking.
Sim-yâ'a§ tûr'dûng. **Tiger alive is.**	The tiger is (*at present*) alive.
Bû'lû â'pô mô'dûng. **They liquor making is.**	They are (*now*) making liquor.
Bui âm‖ yik'dûng. **She dhan treading is.**	She is (*now*) treading out the dhan.
Ala â'mî a la â'sî‡ tü'-dûng. **That (there) man that water drinking is.**	That man (there) is (*at present*) drinking water.

* ki'na=adjective (sick people).

† Interrogative of verb.

‡ A sort of causal verb.

§ Nominatival "a."

‖ Here the accusative case suffix "em" is omitted for no apparent reason.

"Dâk" generally signifies *to be*, *to become*, *to have*, &c., and appears to differ somewhat in *force* from "dûng"; as—

EXAMPLES.

Â-sî'a* tê'dâng	The water is rising.
Â-sî'a* â'dâk	The water is falling.
Â-sî'a* gû'dâk	The water is hot.
Gâ-sôr'a* bî-sâm'dâk........................	The cloth is coarse.
Gâ-sôr'a* bâ-sôr'dâk	The cloth is fine.
Ngâ'ka yô-gôn'a* bâ-tê'dâk	My bag is large.
Dâ'muir muir'dâk	It is thundering.
Sî û'kâ sî gur'dâk	This stick is crooked.
Sî â'mî sî tôr'dâk	This man is strong.
Bui rû-bê'dâk........................	He is deaf.
Bui mû'jî dâk	He is old.
Bui yâ-mê'dâk He young is	He is young.
Bui kân-kân'dâk She pretty is	She is pretty.

"Dûng" and "dâk," however, appear to be *interchangeable*, and this renders it difficult to determine with *certainty* how each should be used. For instance, the whole of the above examples might be equally correctly rendered with "dûng" (though it is *more usual* to use "dâk") and here follow some more examples where *either* could be used; as :—

EXAMPLES.

Mô'tê dâk *or* dûng. Far is.	It is far.
Pô'dông ô'dâk *or* dûng. Rain falling is.	It is raining.
Dâ'mûm dâk *or* dûng. Cloudy is.	It is cloudy.
Bue jîr'dâk *or* dûng. He angry is.	He is angry.
Bui kâ-lik-shû'†dâk *or* dûng. He pleased is.	He is pleased.

"Dâk" and "dûng" are sometimes used in the *past* sense to denote something which has recently happened; as—

EXAMPLES.

Â-mî'a* gî-â'dâk. Man come has.	A man has just come.

* Nominatival "a."

† Reflective particle.

Another noticeable feature about these auxiliary verbs is that "dûng" and "dâk" often change into "dâng" when *interrogatively* used; as—

EXAMPLES.

É-lûng'a* pui-dâng-na'yü ? † Boat arrived has ?	Has the boat arrived (or not) ?
Êlûng'a* adit'kå bå-då-dâng'na ? Boat how much long is ?	What length is the boat ?
Nå in'kom mui-dâng'na ? You what requiring are ?	What do you want ?
Nå in'kom bom-dâng'na ? You what brought ?	What have you brought?
Bui in'kom lû-dâng'na ? He what said has ?	What did he say ?

As the first of the examples given *overleaf* might be equally correctly rendered as follows:—

Ê-lûng'a pui-dâk-vô'yü ? Ê-lûng'a pui-dû-vô'yü ?	lit., Is the arrival of the boat an affair of the past ?

I am led to believe that "dàng" is used to denote *past time* generally just as "kàng" (*vide* page 83 *post*) is with root verbs. The correct rendering of "ê-lûng'a pui-dâng-na'yü ?" being "the boat has arrived" (has it not ?) for "yü" is decidedly an interrogative *alternative* particle. So the correct rendering of "ê-lûng'a a-dit'kå bå-då-dâng'na ?" is most likely "how long did the boat turn out ?" and this supposition is strengthened by the Miri rendering of "what have you brought?" *viz.*, "na in'kom bom-dâng'na ?" It is further strengthened too by the fact that examples Nos. 3 and 5 above are often rendered with "in-kå'kå" instead of "in-kom," the correct English interpretation of the two sentences in question *then* being "of what have you desired ?" (No. 3), and "of what has he spoken ?" (No. 5).

"Dûng" (and "dâk") may be and often is abbreviated to "dû," and "då," the first being used, in conjunction with "dî," a particle denoting *vague probability*, when *asking questions*, and the latter "då"‡ to express *indefinite* present time, or to express *habit*, *custom*, &c., as—

EXAMPLES.

Bui	teng'ûr	shû§-dû'dî ?	Can he be drunk ? (*i.e.*, is it possible that he is ?)
He	drunk	is ?	

* Nominatival "a."

† "yü" interrogative alternative particle.

‡ *Vide* the miscellaneous for examples showing how repeatedly "då" is used in conversation.

§ "shû" is a reflective particle only.

Âm-buin'lâ kê'bûng dû'dî? Rice in mice are?	Is it possible there are mice in the rice?
Pô'dông ô-dû'dî ô-mâ'dî? Rain falling is falling not?	Can it be raining, or not?
Nâ'lû Mî-shing'a* â-pông'em tü-dâ'yü You Miris liquor drink?	Do you Miris drink liquor?
A ngâ'lû tü'dâ Yes, we drink (it).	Yes, we drink (it).
Tâ-buî'a* pâ'dâ Snakes strike	Snakes sting.
Pret-tang'a* bêr'dâ Birds fly	Birds fly.
Nâ tât-ken-dâ'yü? You understand	Do you understand.
A tât-ken'dâ Yes, understand	Yes, I understand.

"dû" and "dâ" are also used with the comparative particle "vô;" as—

EXAMPLES.

Ê-lûng'a† pui-dû-vo'yü?	Has the boat arrived?
E-lung'a† pui-dâ'vong	The boat has arrived.

N.B.—The "da" noticed above is equivalent to the Kachari present tense affix "ŭ."

CONJUGATIONAL EXAMPLES.

Verb "to see" (ka"=see, "look," root).

INDICATIVE MOOD.

PRESENT TENSE.

The present tense is formed by adding "dûng" or "dâk," the present of the substantive verbs, to the root, as—

Singular.	*Plural.*
Ngâ kâ'dûng *or* dâk. I see.	Ngâ'lû kâ'dûng *or* dâk. we see.
Nâ kâ'dûng *or* dâk. thou seest.	Nâ'lû kâ'dûng *or* dâk.. you see.
Bui kâ'dûng *or* dâk. he or she sees.	Bû'lû kâ'dûng *or* dâk.. they see.

The present definite is formed by adding "lâ" (the participial suffix) to the root, followed by "dûng" or "dâk"—

PRESENT DEFINITE.

Singular.	*Plural.*
Ngâ kâ-lâ'dûng *or* dâk.. I am seeing.	Ngâ'lû kâ-lâ'dûng *or* dâk.. we are seeing.
Nâ kâ-lâ'dûng *or* dâk.. thou art seeing.	Nâ'lû kâ-lâ'dûng *or* dâk.. you are seeing.
Bui kâ-lâ'dûng *or* dâk.. he or she is seeing.	Bû'lû kâ-lâ'dûng *or* dâk., they are seeing.

* Nominatival "a."

EXAMPLES.

Kô bui yûv-lâ dûng. Child he sleeping is.	The child is sleeping.
Nå'ka gî-â-då'dem ngå yûv-lâ-dûng'ai Your coming time of I sleeping was	I was sleeping when you came.
Bû'lû mâk'shå kâ-lâ'dûng. They dancing looking are.	They are looking at the dancing.
Bû'lû ê'ek bå-lâ'dûng. They pig singing are.	They are singing the pig.

N.B.—From the examples given above it will be observed that this tense is used to express a *present* act or event which is not yet *completed.*

The imperfect tense is formed by adding "tû'ai" to the root, as—

IMPERFECT TENSE.

Singular.		*Plural.*	
Ngå kâ-tû'ai......	I saw.	Nga'lû kâ-tû'ai...	we saw.
Nå kâ-tû'ai......	thou sawest.	Na'lû kâ-tû'ai...	you saw.
Bui kâ-tû'ai ...	he or she saw.	Bû'lû kâ-tû'ai...	they saw.

EXAMPLES.

Â-mî'ka kâ-tû'ai, sî da kû. Man a saw, this he verily.	I saw a man, this is he (*i.e.*, this is the man whom I saw).
Kô'la ngâ då-tû'ai. Childhood I ate	I ate it in childhood.

The imperfect definite represents the action or event as remaining *unfinished* at a certain *past* time. It is compounded of the *root* and the *past tense* of the *substantive verb* ; as—

IMPERFECT DEFINITE.

Singular.	*Plural.*
Ngå kâ-dûng'ai, *or* dâg'ai* I was seeing	Ngå lû kâ-dûng'ai *or* dâg'ai. we were seeing.
Nå kâ-dûng'ai *or* dâg'ai. thou wert seeing.	Nå'lû kâ-dûng'ai *or* dâg'ai. you were seeing.
Bui kâ-dûng'ai *or* dâg'ai . he or she was seeing.	Bû'lû kâdûng'ai *or* dâg'ai. they were seeing.

EXAMPLES.

Nå'ka gî-â-då'dem bui ngôm pâ-dûng'ai. Your coming time of he me striking was	He was striking me when you came.
E'lûng pur-lik'då'dem â'mî ê-ing'kå â-râ'lâ dûng'ai Boat upset time of men ten inside were	There were ten men in the boat when it upset.

---

* "g" is substituted for "k" merely for the sake of euphony.

The perfect tense is formed by adding "tô" to the root; as—

PERFECT TENSE.

Singular.		*Plural.*	
Ngâ kâ'tô ...	I have seen.	Ngâ'lû kâ'tô...	We have seen.
Nâ kâ'tô ...	You have seen.	Nâ'lû kâ'tô ...	You have seen.
Bui kâ'tô ...	He or she has seen.	Bû'lû kâ'to ...	They have seen.

With certain verbs the third person singular and plural of this tense is formed by an *alternative* suffix, "kâng" *generally*, to denote *distant* past time, as—

EXAMPLES.

Ê-ngâ'a * yû'kâng. Fish rotten.	The fish is (has become) rotten.
Pret-tâng'a * bêr'kâng. Bird flown.	The bird has flown.
Bui gî-kâng'kû. He departed.	He has departed.
Bui sî'kâng. He dead.	He has breathed his last.
Bui ai-rû'pü shông'kâng. He very thin.	He has become very thin.
Bet'kâng. Broken.	(It is) broken.
U-mü'a * mit'kâng. Fire gone out.	The fire has gone out.
Yôk'kâng. Lost.	(It is) lost.
E-lûng'a * â-sî'lâ jin-âng'kâng. Boat water in sunk.	The boat has sunk (in the water).
Sî û'kâ sî bet'kâng. This stick this broken.	This stick is broken.
A-sî'lâ ô-lek'kâng. Water in fallen.	(It) has fallen into the water.

As I have said above, "kâng" is used *generally* to denote *distant past* time. It is not, however, *invariably* so used; as—

EXAMPLES.

Bui sû'pâk gî'kâng. He now gone.	He has just gone. (Assam—hi ê-ti'â gôl)

"Kâng" may be, and often is, *abbreviated* to "kâ," and in its *abbreviated* form it appears to be used with all verbs, and with

* Nominatival "a."

the first, second, or third persons. It is, in fact, in its *abbreviated* form, a sort of pluperfect tense suffix, as—

EXAMPLES.

Nå'ka gî-ro'sim bå'jê pô'dông ô'kâ. Your departure after much rain fell.	Much rain fell after your departure.
Bui ma'yŭm så åpin då'kå. He last evening here rice eaten had.	He ate rice here last evening.
Lông'a ko-nâng'kå idå vôdê?* Days nine expired?	Can nine days have expired?
Nå då-lû'lå gî-kå'yü? You village to gone had?	Had you gone to the village?
Nå'kå gi-å'då'dem † ngå gî'kå. Your coming time of I had gone.	I had gone when you came.
Bui sî-kå'dî? He die had?	Can he have died?
Bû'lû nôm må-tå-kå'püǂ gî-âng'kå. They you searching purpose of came had.	They had come to search for you.

The future (implying a *determination*) tense is formed by adding "yê" to the root as—

FUTURE TENSE.

Singular.		*Plural.*	
Ngå kå'yê ...	I shall see.	Ngå'lû kå'yê..	We shall see.
Nå kå'yê ...	Thou shalt see.	Nå'lû kå'yê..	You shall see.
Bui kå'yê ...	He, or she, shall see.	Bui'lû kå'yê..	They shall see.

EXAMPLES.

Pô'dông ô'yê Rain fall will	It will rain (at once or very shortly).
Ngå gî'yê. I go will.	I shall go (at once).
Ngå yüv'yê. I sleep will.	I shall sleep (ditto).
Nå a-dî'lô gî'yê'na? You when go will?	When shall you go.
Nå ngôm a-dî'lô bî yê'na? You me to when give will?	When will you give it to me?
Då'rê-yê Sun shine will	The sun will shine (at once or very shortly).

* "vô" completive particle, "dê" particle of vague probability.

† "gê-å-då'dem"=adverbial participle of root verb "gî-â"=come.

ǂ "mâ-tâ-ka'pü"=infinitive of purpose of root verb "mâ'ta"= search for.

When it is intended to express a *doubtful* future *contingency*, the particle "dì" (signifying *vague probability*) is affixed to the future tense suffix "yê." When so affixed "yê'dì" is *interrogative*, or well as *indefinitely* affirmative, as—

EXAMPLES.

Pô'dông ô-yê'dì.	It will probably rain. Will it be likely to rain?
Bui gì-â-yê'dì.	He will probably come. Will he be likely to come?
Au ô-yê'dì ô-mâ-yê'dì ngâ **Son born will born not will** I **kâ'pü*** ken-yê'na? **how** know shall?	How shall I tell whether a son will be born or not?

The future tense may also be made by adding the particle "pü" (denoting *probability*.) to the root, as—

EXAMPLES.

Ngâ gì'pü. **I go will.**	**I will go.**
Ngâ nôm pâ'pü. **I you beat will.**	I will beat you.
Nâ a-dì'lô gì-pui'â?† **You when go will?**	**When will you go?**
Ngâ nôm dôk-shì-rì'kâ bì pü. **I you necklace give** will.	**I will give you a necklace.**

This particle "pü" is also very largely used (in the above sense) in conjunction with the *true* tense suffix "yê," as—

EXAMPLES.

Pô'dông ô-yê'pü. **Rain fall will.**	**It will (possibly) rain.**
Dâ-rê'mui'lô ai'rûp âng-kìr-yê'pü. **Sunshine if very warm will (be).**	**If the sun shines it will (probably) be very warm.**
Bû'lû mâk'shâ shâ-mân-yê'pü. **They dance will.**	**They will (likely) dance.**
Nâ buim yâm'pô kâ-veg-yê'pü. **You him morrow see able will (be).**	**You will (likely) see him to-morrow.**
Nâ'ka tâ ra ai-yê'pü. **Your sore well will (get).**	**Your sore will get well.**
Sâk ka polo me lam sâ Kam-tì'a a'm-buin'em bom yê pü.	**The Khámptis will bring in rice next month.**
Bû'lû lô ê-ì'lâ âm'em gâ-yê'pü. **They days ten in "dhan" cut will.**	**They will cut their "dhan" in ten days' time.**

---

* **Kâ'pü**=adverb, in what manner, or way?

† **This** "i" is merely added for the sake of euphony.

"Pü" is also used in conjunction with another particle, "kü" (which is I believe the *affirmative* particle "kû," *softened* to "kü" for the *sake of euphony*), but only in the third person singular and plural, as—

EXAMPLES.

Tâng'a* nâ'ka gâ-sôr'em shâ-pet-† pü'kü. Thorns your cloth tear will.	The thorns will tear your clothes.
Ê-kî'a* nôm rok-pü'kü. Dog you bite will.	The dog will bite you.
Bû'lû nôm pâ-pükü. They you beat will.	They will beat you.
Ô-lek-pükü. Fall will.	It will fall.
Bet-pü'kü. Break will.	It will break.
Âm'em ai-ô'pü kâ-mâ'mui"lô men-jâk'a dâ-pü'kü. Dhan well see not if buffaloes eat will.	If (you) do not watch the "dhan" well the buffaloes will eat it.

The imperfect (future) tense is formed by adding the particle "pü," in conjunction with "ai," the sign of the past tense of the substantive verb, to the root, as—

IMPERFECT TENSE.

Singular.		*Plural.*	
Ngâ kâ'-pui'‡ai	... I would see.	Ngâ'lû kâ-pui'ai	... we would see.
Nâ kâ-pui'ai	... thou would'st see.	Nâ'lû kâ-pui'ai	.. you would se
Bui kâ-pui'ai	... he, or she, would see.	Bû'lû kâ-pui'ai	... they would see.

EXAMPLE.

Pô'dông ô-mâ'mui"lô ngâ gi-gâ-pui'ai. Rain fall not if I stroll would.	If it did not rain, I would go for a stroll.

POTENTIAL MOOD.

The present tense is formed by adding "lâ" (the present participial suffix) and "pü" (the particle denoting *probability*

---

* Nominatival "a."

† Shâ-pet=compound verb, "shâ"=pull, "pet"=tear (*i.e.*, to tear by a pulling process).

‡ This "i" is merely euphonic.

noticed *ante*) to the root, as—

PRESENT TENSE.

Singular.		*Plural.*	
Ngâ kâ-lâ'pü	... I am able to see.	Ngâ'lû kâ-lâ'pü	... we are able to see.
Nâ kâ-lâ'pü	... you are able to see.	Nâ'lû kâ-lâ'pü	... you are able to see.
Bui kâ-lâ'pü	... he, or she, is able to see.	Bû'lû kâ-lâ'pü	... they are able to see.

Miris have a particle, "veg," which is apparently equivalent to the English auxiliary verb *can*, though it is much more *restricted* in its use, for it is only heard with the verbs to *see*, *hear*, and *smell*, but with these verbs it is used in *lieu* of "lâ'pü" in the *present*, *past*, and *future* tenses of the *potential* and *subjunctive* moods, as—

EXAMPLE.

Nâ kâ-veg-dâ'yü? You see can?	Can you see (it)?
A! kâ-veg'dûng (*or* "dâk," *or* "dâ".) Yes! see can.	Yes! I can see.
Ngâ'ka â'gôm lû-nâm'em* tât-beg-tô'yü? My speaking hear able have?	Did you hear me speaking?
A! tât-beg'tô. Yes! heard have.	Yes! I heard (you).
Yâ'na ê'ngâ â-rü'em nâm-veg-dû'yü? Rotten fish smell smell able are?	Can you smell the rotten fish.
Mâ! ngâ nâm-veg'mâ. No! I smell can not.	No! I cannot smell.

ILLUSTRATIVE SENTENCES WITH "*lâ'pu.*"

Nâ â-tè'rê sim dî'bâ sim jô-sâ-lâ-pui'â? You alone this bamboo this lift able are?	Are you able to lift this bamboo alone.
Ngâ jô-sâ-lâ'mâ. I lift able not.	I am not able to lift (it).

* Past participle of verb "lû" = speak, with accusative case suffix "em" attached, here used as a verbal noun.

Yâm'pô nâ-ka'lâ buim Morrow you along with him gî-vô*-lâ-pü'mui"lô accompany able will if gî-vô-lâng'kâ. accompany permit.	If you will be able to bring him with you to-morrow, do so.
Â-lâ'mâng. Write able not.	I am not able to write.
Â'sî kâ-mâng†-kô'lâ ê'ngâ tûr- Waterless place in fish live lâ'mâ. able not.	Fish cannot live out of water (*lit.*, in a waterless place).

Desire is *generally* expressed by the use of the verb "mui" = *desire, wish*; but there are likewise two *desiderative* particles which are largely used (*vide* page 101, *post*), as—

EXAMPLES.

Ngâ gi'pü mui'dûng. I go to wish.	I wish to go.
Bui nâ-ka'lâ â-gôm'em lû'pü He your with words say to mui'dûng. wishes.	He wishes to speak with you.
Ni'tôm mô-nâm'em‡ tât'pü Singing hear to mui'dûng. wish.	I wish to hear the singing.
Nâ kâ-pî'lâ bâzâr'lâ gi'pü You why bazar in go to mui-dû'na? wish?	Why do you wish to go into the bazar?

The past (imperfect) tense is formed by adding "lâ-pui'ai" to the root, as—

PAST TENSE.

Singular.	*Plural.*
Ngâ kâ-lâ-pui'§ai... I could see.	Ngâ'lu kâ-lâ-pui'ai ... we could see.
Nâ kâ-lâ-pui'ai... thou could'st see.	Nâ'lû kâ-lâ-pui'ai ... you could see.
Bui kâ-lâ-pui'ai ... he, or she, could see.	Bû' la kâ-lâ-pui'ai ... they could see.

---

* "vô" particle denoting accompaniment, "gî-vô'to-kâ" = escort, take *with*, &c.

† "kâ mâng" = exists not, "kô" = place.

‡ Past participle passive of root verb "mô" = make, with accusative case suffix "em" attached, making "mô-nam'em" a verbal noun.

§ This extra "i" is merely euphonic.

Examples.

Dá'mûm mâ-mui'lô ngâ'lû pô-lô'em Clouds not if we moon * kâ-lâ-pui'ai. see able could.	If there were no clouds we could see the moon.
E'ngâ ai-mui'lô ngâ Fish good had been if I dâ-lâ-pui'ai eat able could.	Had the fish been good I could have eaten it.
Bû lû ngôm lû-lâ-pü'mâng"ai They me say able to not was.	They could not tell me.

The future tense is formed by adding "lâ-ye'pü" to the root, as—

Simple Future

Singular.		*Plural.*	
Ngâ kâ-lâ-yê'pü ...	I shall be able to see.	Ngâlû-kâ-lâ-yê'pü ...	we shall be able to see.
Nâ kâ-lâ-yê'pü ...	you will be able to see.	Nâlû kâ-lâ-yê'pü ...	you will be able to see.
Bui kâ-lâ-yê'pü ...	he, or she, will be able to see.	Bû'lû kâ-lâ-yê'pü ...	they will be able to see.

Examples.

Yâm-pô'yûm ngâlû pô-lô'em Morrow evening we moon kâ†-lâ-yêpü see able will.	We shall be able to see the moon to-morrow evening.
Nâ â-pôngem bâ-jêkâ bî-muilô You liquor much give if ngâlu yâ yâ-bung'em mak'shâ we night night long dance shâ-lâ-yê'pü able will.	If you give us plenty of liquor, we shall be able to dance all night.

Subjunctive Mood.

The present tense is formed by adding "mui'lô" = *if* to the root, as—

Present Tense.

Singular.		*Plural.*	
Ngâ kâ-mui'lô...	if I see.	Ngâ'lû kâ-mui'lô...	if we see.
Nâ kâ-mui'lô ...	if you see.	Nâ'lû kâ-mui'lô ...	if you see.
Bui kâ-mui'lô ...	if he, or she, sees.	Bû'lû kâ-mui'lô ...	if they see.

---

* kâ-veg-lâ pui'ai *or* kâ-veg-pui'ai *or* kâ-pui'ai may likewise be used.

† *Or* kâ-veg-yê'pü.

(N.B.—This tense may likewise be formed by a particle, "em," attached to root.)

EXAMPLES.

È-kum'a* dâ'dî dî-dû'mui"lô House leak is if tâ'sê ân-jâ'kâ kâp-tem-tô-kû'kâ.† thatching-grass little put on.	If the house leaks, put on a little thatch.
Nâ da'pü î-mui'lô pâ-pü-lâng'â. You thus do if get will not.	If you do so, you cannot obtain it.
Bui gî'pü mui-dû'mui"lô gi-mô'tokâ He go to wish is if go permit.	If he wishes to go, let him go.
Ngâ mai-nâm'pü lû-tô'mui"lô nâ I falsely spoken have if you ken-yê'pü. know will.	If I have told a lie, you will know.
Buim kâ-mui'lô lû'pü. Him see if say will.	I will tell him, if I see him.

The past tense is formed by adding "â-mui'lô" (the "â" is I believe an abbreviation of the "kâ" alluded to *ante*) to the root, to which with *some* verbs "ng" must be *first* added for the sake of euphony, as—

PAST TENSE.

Singular.	*Plural.*
Ngâ kâng-â'mui"lô... if I had seen.	Ngâ'lû kâng-â'mui"lô... if we had seen.
Nâ kâng-â'mui"lô ... if thou hadst seen.	Nâ'lû kâng-â'mui"lô ... if you had seen.
Bui kâng-â'mui"lô ... if he, or she, had seen.	Bû'lû kâng-â'mui"lô ... if they had seen.

That the "ng" is used merely to prevent the hiatus is, I think, manifest from the fact that many verbs do not require it. For instance, "If I had *gone*" would be "Ngâ gî-â'mui"lo" while "if I had *heard*" would be "Ngâ tâd-â'mui"lô" the "d" (*hear* is "tât'to-kâ") being substituted for "t" also to prevent the hiatus.

EXAMPLES.

Sim yông'mô sim dâ-â'mui"lô ngâ This poison this eat had if I sî-pui'ai. die would.	Had I eaten this poison, I would have died.
Lâm-bü'lâ yûm'râ mâng-â'mui"lô Road on jungle not been had if ngâ gi-pui'ai. I go would.	Had there been no jungle on the road I would have gone.

* Nominatival "a."

† Affirmative particle.

Nâ ân-jâ'kâ teng-â'mui"lô buim You little hurry had if him rik-shû-pui'ai.* met would.	Had you hurried a little, you would have met him.
Sî û'kâ sî ân-dâ-yâng-â'mui"lô† This stick this shorter had if ngâ-ka'pü ai-pui'ai. me for good would.	If this stick had been shorter, it would have suited me.

The future tense is formed by adding "mui'lô" to the future tense suffix "yê," as—

FUTURE TENSE.

Singular.	*Plural.*
Ngâ kâ-yê'mui"lô... if I shall see.	Ngâ'lû kâ-yê'mui"lô... if we shall see.
Na kâ-yê'mui"lô ... if you shall see.	Nâ'lû kâ-yê'mui"lô ... if you will see.
Bui kâ-yê'mui"lô ... if he, or she, will see.	Bû'lû kâ-yê'mui"lô ... if they will see.

EXAMPLES.

Ngâ sâ tâng-nyî'kâ dû-yê'mui"lô I here years two stay shall if Mi'shing â-gôm'em ken-yê'pü. Miri language understand shall.	If I shall stay here two years, I shall know Miri.

MORE EXAMPLES OF HYPOTHETICAL SENTENCES, AFFIRMATIVE AND NEGATIVE.

Ngâ sî-mon'em kâ-mui'lô‡ âp'dâ. I deer see if shoot.	If I see a deer, I shoot it.
Ngâ buim kâ-mui'lô‡ lû'pü. I him see if say will.	If I see him, I will tell him.
Kôn'nô§ ma'lô ngâ Sâ-heb'em kâ- Formerly I Saheb see yê'mui"lô dûg-gôr-dûng'ai. shall if running fast was.	Formerly, if I saw a Saheb, I ran away.
Ngâ buim kâ-to'mui"lô lû-pui'ai. I him see have if say would.	If I saw him, I would tell him.
Ngâ buim kâng-â'mui"lô lû-pui'ai. I him seen had if say would.	If I had seen him, I would have told you.
Ngâ dâ-rep-lâ'mui"lô nôm kâ'pü. I get up able if you see will.	If I can rise, I will see you.

* "shû" = reflective pronoun.

† "yâng" is the comparative adjectival sign "yâ" with "ng" added.

‡ Miris, as a rule, prefer using "kâ-yê'mui"lô."

§ "kôn'nô" = (lit.) day before yesterday, "ma'lô" = yesterday, but "kôn'nô ma'lô" is used as above to denote recently. If it is intended to refer to a greater lapse of time, greater stress is laid on the final syllables of the two words, *viz.*, on "nô" and "lô," especially upon the latter.

Ngâ dâ-rep-lâng-â'mui"lô pâ- I got up able was if beat pui'ai. would.	If I could get up I would beat you.
Ngâ buim kâ-mâ'mui"lô gî-lât-kû'- I him see not if return pü. will.	If I do not see him, I will return.
Pô'dông ô-mâ-dâ'dem* ngâ Rain fall not whilst I in-gem'lâ yûp-tî-dûng'ai. outside sleeping always was.	If it did not rain, I used to sleep outside.
Ngâ buim kâ-mâng-â'mui"lô gî-lât- I him see not had if return pui'ai. would.	If I had not seen him, I would have returned.

Imperative Mood.

The imperative mood is confined in its application to the *second* person singular and plural, and to the *third* person plural *only*; as—

Kâ'to-kâ=see *thou*, once.
Kâ-lâng'kâ= see *thou*, as a rule.
Kâ-tô-î'kâ= *see to*, look after.
Kâ-lâ'jê=let *us* see, or look.

The latter ("kâ-lâ'jê") is more an *exhortation* than a *command*, and in *this sense* "lâ'jê" may be used with *all* verbs. Miris have also a permissive particle "mô"† which is *likewise* used in *that sense* as a sort of auxiliary (like the English word let) in the imperative mood, for the third person singular, and plural; and with "î" added to it for the *first* person singular and plural, as—

Examples.

Buim gî-â-mô'to-kâ. Him come permit.	Let (*permit*) him come.
Ngôm kâ-mô-î'ka. Me see allow.	Let me (*permit*) see.
Ngâ'lûm kâ-mô-î'kâ. Us see allow.	Let us (*permit*) see.

N.B.—The "î" is only used for the second person. Another favourite expression used for the first person is "ngâ kâng-kî-tô'shâ," or "kâ-tô'shâ, ngâ î-kî-tô'shâ," or "î-tô'shâ, ngâ tüng-

* "ô-dâ'dem"=adverbial participle of root verb "ô"=fall, with negative particle "mâ,"=not, attached to root.

† "mô" is also used for making causative verbs, *vide* page 107 *post*.

kî-tô'shâ," or "tü-tô'shâ"=Assamese "sâ-bô-lî dî'bî, kô-rî'â sâm," and "kâ-î'â sâm," respectively.

Yôk'shik dem kâng-kî-tô'shâ (*or* kâ-to'shâ.) Knife it look at. } Let (me) see (*i.e.*, look at) the knife.

The sentence could also be rendered thus:—

Yôk'shik dem kâ-mo-î-kâ. Knife it see cause (to). } Show (me) the knife.
Bui in'quom kâng-ken-ma'nâ? He what know not? } What does he not know?
Â-puing'em kâng-ken'dâ. Everything knows. } He knows everything.

Miris (and Abors likewise) have no way of expressing the *necessity* of an act except by using the Assamese word "lâ'gê." They are probably too democratic to own such a word of their own, but whatever the reason be, "lâ'gê" is the *only* word used; as—

Nâ gî'pü lâ-gî'dâ. You go to necessary is. } You must go.

Perhaps the nearest approach to anything of the kind is the Miri particle "kân"=*fit*, *proper*, which is *only* used in conjunction with the abbreviated form "dû" (*vide ante*) of the substantive verb, and "ai," the sign of the past tense, making "kân-dû'ai"=*lit.*, *fit*, or *proper was*:—

EXAMPLES.

Bui mai-nâ'pü gî-âng-kân-dû'ai. He quickly come proper was. } He ought to have come earlier.
Ngâ'lû sâ-heb'em kâng-kâ'pü gî-kân-dû'ai. We saheb see purpose of go fit was. } We ought (it behoveth us) to go and see the saheb.

They have another particle, *viz.*, "pâ," signifying *right*, which used in conjunction with the negative particle "mâ" becomes "pâ mâ"=*lit.*, right not, *i.e.*, *wrong*, and is then equivalent to the Assamese "nâ pai" ("sûr kô-rî'bô nâ pai"=it is *wrong* to steal); but this is as far off the English word *must* as ever; as—

EXAMPLES.

Nâ mai'nâm â-gôm'em lû-pâ'mâ. You false words speak right not. } You must not tell a lie. (Assamese "toi mî'sâ kô'thâ kô'bô nâ pai.")

The *prohibitive* form is made by adding "yô-kâ" (in *lieu* of "to-kâ") to the root, as—

EXAMPLES.

Kâ'yô-kâ ...	...	... look not.
Yüv'vô-kâ...	...	... sleep not.
Dâ'yô'kâ ...	...	... eat not.
Gi'yô'kâ ...	...	... go not.
&c.		&c.

"Yô-kâ" may be *intensified* by placing the particle "vong" *between* the two syllables; as—

EXAMPLES.

Yüv-yô'vông"kâ	...	... sleep no more.
Bi-yô'vông"kâ	...	... give no more.
Tü-yô'vong"kâ	...	... drink no more.
Ni'tom mô'yô-vong"kâ...		... sing no more.
&c.		&c.

INFINITIVE MOOD.

The infinitive *of purpose* is "kâ'pü," added to the root, as—

EXAMPLES.

Bui ê-lûng'em kâng-kâpü gi'kâng. He boat see purpose gone.	He has gone (for) to see the boat.
Bui â'si tô-kâ'pü gi'kâng. He water bring purpose of gone.	He has gone (for) to felch water.
Bui ê-ngâ'em rê-kâ'pü gi'dûng. She fish buy purpose of gone.	She is going (for) to buy fish.
Mâk'shâ shâ-nâm'em kâng-kâ'pü gi'yô-kâ. Dancing see purpose of go not.	Do not go (for) to see the dancing.
Ngâ'lû pui-gâ'lâ ür-shû-kâ' pü gi-lâ'jê. We "ghat" to bathe purpose of go let.	Let us go to the "ghat" (for) to bathe.

The infinitive is also made by using the particle "pü" (alluded to *ante*), as—

EXAMPLES.

Ngâ gi'pü mui'dûng. I go will wishing am.	I wish to go.
Nâ tü'pü mui-mui'lô tü-lâng'kâ. You drink will wish if drink.	If you wish to drink, do so.

Bâ-zâr'lâ ê'ngâ dû'dî dû-mâ'dî Bázár in fish be be not â-mî'kâ kâ-yê'pü lû-lik'to-kâ. man see will send.	Send a man to see if there are fowls in the bázár or not.
Ngôm bî'pü em'nâ* bôm-â-tô' Me to give will saying brought yü? have?	Did you bring it to give to me.

also by adding the *desiderative* adjectival particle "linga," = *desirous*, to the root, as—

EXAMPLES.

Ngâ buim kâ-ling'a. I him see desirous.	I *wish* to see him.
Ngâ mâk'shâ shâ-nâm'em kâ-ling'a. I dancing see desirous.	I am *desirous* to see the dancing.
Nâ â'pô tü-lî-dü'yü? You liquor drink desirous are?	Do you *desire* to drink liquor?
Ngâ yüv-ling'a. I sleep desirous.	I *wish* to sleep.

PARTICIPLES.

Kâ-dû'em *or* Kâ-dâ'dem	(Whilst) seeing.
Kâng'kôm	Seeing (notwithstanding I see).
Kâ'lâ	Having seen (conjunctive).
Kâ'nâm	Seen (past passive).
Kâ'na	One who sees, seer.
Kâtî'lâ, kâ-tî'lâ	Continuing to see.

The adverbial participle in "dâ'dem" is largely used, as—

EXAMPLES.

Nâ'ka yüp-dâ'dem bâ'jê pô'dông Your sleeping whilst much rain ôkâ. fell.	Much rain fell while you were sleeping.
Â'pin mô-dâ'dem ê-kum'lâ Rice cooking whilst house to ümü ükâng. fire burnt.	Whilst cooking the house was burnt.

The present participle in "kôm" is also largely used, as—

EXAMPLES.

Sû'pâk bî'kôm ai'dâ. Now giving good is.	Now giving good, *i.e.*, I should like it now.

* Past participle, with "na" substituted for "l" for sake of euphony.

Pâ-muin*-shû-dâk'kôm Striking gê-muin*-shû-dâk-kôm â-kâm'a. quarrelling same.	Striking and fighting (one with another) is the same (thing).
Sâ dâk'kôm â'pin mô'pü Here being food cook will.	Being here I will cook.
Sû'pâk mâk'shâ kâng'kôm ai dâk. Now dance seeing well is.	It would be well to see the dancing now.
Dâ-gâd†-dâk'kôm Eat disinclined being Dâ-gâd†-mâng'kôm nâ eat disinclined not being you dâ-kân-dû'ai. eat ought.	Whether inclined to eat or not, you ought to eat.

The present participle in "lá" is *indefinite*; as—

EXAMPLES.

Bui gî'lâ kâtô. He gone having saw.	He went and saw.
Ngâ dâ'lâ gî-âng-kû‡'pü. I eat having come again will.	I will eat and come again.
Bui lô-nyî'kâ dûng-gê'lâ gî-kû pü. He days two stay having return will.	Having stayed two days he will return.
Dâ-pî-ô'nem ât-târ'em â-puing'em Stolen goods all lur-shû'lâ dûk-kâng'kû§. hide having ran off.	Having hid what (he) had stolen (he) ran off.
Bui da'pü lû'lâ gî-kâng'kû§. He thus speak having departed.	Having thus spoken he departed.

The past (passive) participle in "nâm" is largely used but *never* in an active sense, as:—

EXAMPLES.

Ngâ'ka kâ'nâm âmi'a.‖ My seen man.	The man I saw, *i.e.*, seen of me.

Vide ante for more examples.

EXAMPLES.

"Kâ'na" is often used to denote the *agent*, or *doer*, of the action expressed by the verb, it answers, in fact, to the Kachari past participle in "nai;" as—

---

* "muin"=is a reciprocative particle, and when used with "shû," the "muin'shû" is used to denote reflective reciprocal action.

† "gâ" is a particle used to denote disinclination, with "d" added for sake of euphony.

‡ This "kû" is a sort of transitive particle, denoting a returning anything, or return to or from a place.

§ This is the affirmative particle.

‖ Nominatival a.

EXAMPLES.

Am pâ'na ki-ding'a * sû pâk â-pin'em dâ'dûng. "Dhan" cutters now rice eating are.	The paddy-cutters are now eating their rice.

VERBAL NOUN.

The past participle in "nâm" is often used as a *verbal noun*, as—

EXAMPLES.

Nâ'ka âb-nâm'a* ai'mâ. Your shooting good not.	Your shooting is bad.
Dû'mai bui nâ'ka âb-nâm†'em ai'dâk em'tô. Dumai he your shooting good is said.	Dumai said your shooting is good.
Nâka ôm-nâma‡ ai-yâdâk. Your sowing better is	Your sowing is better.
Nâ'ka shâben mâ‖-tâ-nâmom sim-yâa dâlo. Your goat searching tiger eaten has.	The tiger has eaten the goat which you are searching for.
Nâka nîtôm mô¶-nâmem lât-gâdâ. Your singing hear disinclined am.	I am tired of hearing your singing.

EXPRESSION OF CAUSE AND EFFECT.

Cause is denoted by affixing the present participal suffix "lâ" to the root verb; as—

EXAMPLES.

Kô'a* kâb'lâ pâ tô. Child cry having beaten have.	I beat the child *because* it was crying.
Pô'dông ô'lâ nâ gî-mâ-na'yü? Rain fallen having you came not?	Was it *because* it rained that you did not come?

Cause may also be denoted by affixing "gâ'lok" to the root; as—

Kô'a* kâb-gâ' lok pâ'to. Child crying from beaten have.	I beat the child *because* it was crying.

---

* Nominatival "a."

† Past participle of root verb "âp" (*p* changed to *b* for sake of euphony)=shoot, with accusative case added.

‡ Ditto with accusative case suffix "em" added.

§ Ditto of root verb "ôm"=sow, with nominatival "a" added.

‖ Ditto root verb "mâta"=search for, with accusative case suffix "em".

¶ Ditto root verb "nitôm-mô"=sing, with accusative case suffix added.

Â-ti-kâ'sin dâ-màng-gâ' Anything at all eating not lok nâ kê-nô'dûng. from you hungry are.	You are hungry, *because* you have eaten nothing.

Effect is denoted by using the adverb "dê-pî'lâ" = *therefore*, as—

EXAMPLES.

Bui kâp-dûng'ai dê-pî'lâ ngâ He crying was, therefore I pâ'tô. beaten have.	He was crying, therefore I beat him.
Lâm'bü bê-lâb-dûng'ai* dê-pî'lâ Road slippery was therefore ô-lek-tô. fallen have.	The road was slippery, therefore I fell.

The following illustrations will show the construction used in Miri after verbs of *asking*, *entreating*, *commanding*, *seeing*, *hearing*, and *feeling*.

EXAMPLES.

Ngâ bui-ka'lok â-bàr'kô I his possession from rupee one kô'tô. solicited.	I asked him for a rupee.
Ngôm mê-lek-yê-kû'pü em'nâ Me release will again saying ngâ kûm'tô. I begged.	I begged him to let me go.
Bui ngôm dû-mô'tô. He me sit caused.	He bade me sit down.
Bui'ka î-dâ'dem ngâ kâ'tô. His doing whilst I saw.	I saw him do it.
Bui'ka lû-dâ'dem ngâ tât'tô. His saying whilst I heard.	I heard him say it.
Ngâ gî'gê mâ lû-dâ'dem ngâ I go will not saying whilst I tât'tô. heard.	I heard him say I will not go.
Ngâ'ka â'lê gûk-dâ'dem ngâ My leg catching whilst I kâng-ken†tô. become aware have.	I felt him catch my leg.

* "Slippery" is "bî-lav'a" the "v" is changed here into a "d" for the sake of euphony.

† "kângken" compound word ("kâ" = *see* "ken" = *know*) avow knowledge of.

Miris have no word for *dare*, "*Dare* you do so and so" would be rendered "are you afraid or not."

13.—Passive Voice.

There is no passive voice in Miri.

14.—Causative Verbs.

Miris have a separate verb for *show*, *viz.*, "len-kân'to-kâ" [len=out (here signifying bringing to open view) "kâ"=see], but all other causal verbs are formed by attaching the root verb "mô,"* =make, to the simple root verbs; as—

EXAMPLES.

Kâ-mô'to-kâ	Cause to see	(kâ=see, mô=make, same as len-kânto-kâ.)
Jü-mô'to-kâ	"	wet (jü=wet).
Gâg-mô'to-kâ..............	"	catch (gâk=catch, *k* changed to *g* for euphony).
Ur-mô'to-kâ	"	bathe. (ür=bathe).
Jir-mo'to-kâ	"	to be angry (jir=anger).
Lâ-mô'to-kâ	"	bring (lâ=bring).
&c.		&c.

If necessary, the several tense suffixes may be added to "mô," and the causative verb declined as a simple one; as—

EXAMPLES.

Mi'ûm ki'dî dem sâ mâk'shâ Girls them here dance shâ-mô'pü. make will.	I will make the girls dance here.
Kô dem jîr-mô'muilo kâv†- Child it cross make if cry ye'pü. will.	If you make the child cross, it will cry.
Nâ buim ma'lô shâ-ben'em You him yesterday goat rin-mô-â'muilo â'lê dîr tie up made had leg break mâng'ai. would not.	Had you made him tie up the goat yesterday, it would not have broken its leg.
Bui bui'ka dôk-shi'rî dem nôm She her necklace it you to kâ-mô-dâk'kôm lâ'yô-kâ. showing take not.	Even if she shows you her necklace, don't take it.
Nâ buim kâ-pi'lâ kâp-mô-tô'yü ? You her why cry make have ?	Why have you made her cry ?

* There is also a permissive particle "mô."
† *v* merely euphonic.

Causative verbs may likewise be formed by adding the particle "yîr," = teach, to the root verb; as—

EXAMPLES.

Lû-yîr' to-kâ	teach to speak.	(lû=speak).
Om-yir' to-kâ	" sow	(ôm=sow).
I-yîr' tô-kâ	" work (generally)	(î=work).
Mâkshâ shâ-yîr'to-kâ ...	" dance	(mâkshâ shâ=dance).
Nîtôm mô-yîr' to-kâ ...	" sing	(nîtôm mô=sing).
&c.,	&c.,	

The tense suffixes may likewise be attached to the above if necessary; as—

EXAMPLES.

Nâ ngôm Mi'shing â-gôm'em You me Miri language lû-yîr-pui'â ? speak teach will ?	Will you teach me Miri ?
Nâ â'pin mô-yîr-kô-shû'pü You food make teach self to lâ-gî'dâ must.	You must learn (teach self) to cook.
Ngâ nôm ôm-yîr-lâ'pü. I you sew teach can.	I can teach you to sew.
Nâ ngôm mâk'shâ shâ-yîr-lâ- You me dancing teach able pü'mui' lo shâ-yîr-î'kâ* if dance teach.	If you can teach me to dance do so.

And lastly a sort of causative is formed by adding a second "kâ" to the imperative suffix "to-ka"; as—

EXAMPLES.

Ur'sing nâ-tô-kâ'kâ † Wood cut go.	Go and cut some wood (Assam. khori kât gûi jâ).
Pô'rôk'â â'pui pui-to'dî'pui-mâ'dî Fowl egg lay has lay not kâ-tô-kâ'kâ† see go.	See if the fowl has laid or not.
Buim gôk-tô-kâ'kâ† em'to-kâ Him call bid (one)	Bid (one) call him.
Tu-tô-lâng-kâ'kâ. Drink go.	Go and drink.
Ngâ â-pin'em dâ-kâ-kû'pu‡ I rice eat go will.	I will go and eat (ing) rice.
Châ ! dâ-tô-lâng-kâ-kû'kâ. Right ! eat go.	All right ! go and eat.

* This "î" is a connective particle.
† " "kâ" ditto.
‡ "dâ-kâ-pu"=infinitive of purpose of root verb "dâ"=eat, with "kû," the particle denoting a returning, added.

The "kâ" can only be used with the *Imperative*, "*I* will send to fetch water" would be—

Ngâ âsi to-mô'pu............ fetch water=toto-kâ.

15.—Compound Verbs.

The *analogous* construction of the Miri and the Kachari language is very marked here, inasmuch as in Miri verbal roots may be compounded (*a*) with other verbal roots; as—

Examples.

Gi-gê-mô'to-kâ=send away (gê=go, gi=scold, with causal "mô").
Lû-bi'to-kâ=explain (lû=speak, bî=give).
Lâ-len'to-kâ=take out of (lâ=take, len=out).
Gê-ki'to-kâ=try on clothes (gê=wear, ki=measure).
Lâ-bi'to-kâ=bring and give (lâ=bring, bî=give).
Yir-kâ'to-kâ=poke fun at (yir=laugh, kâ=see).
Dâ-ki'to-kâ=taste food (dâ=eat, ki=measure).
Tüng-ki'to-kâ=taste liquids (tu=drink, kî=measure).
&c., &c.

In such compounds, too, the *second* root, to quote the Revd. Mr. Endle (page 27 of his Kachari Grammar) often indicates the result of the compound action indicated by the whole verb, while the former root shows the manner in which this result is brought about," thus:—

Mô-kê'to-kâ=kill (generally, *i.e.*, by any means).
Din-kê'to-kâ=beat, with stick or wood } to death.
Nik-kê'to-kâ=pierce, with some piercing weapon } to death.
Pâ-kê'to-kâ=cut, with any weapon } to death.
Âp-kê'to-kâ=shoot, with gun, or bow and arrow } to death.

(*b*) With various particles, the most *common* of which are—

mûr=mistake, oversight (generally used in conjunction with reflective particle "shû.")
mân=fun, play.
rik=meet, *i.e.*, come together.
âm=every one, whole number of, &c.
vô=completion, sometimes preparedness, &c.
pô=priority.
pui=sufficiency, also arrival at destination, &c.
lât=a returning of things, also to, or from, a place &c. (generally used in conjunction with particle "kâ").
kû=returning from a journey, also returning of things (this particle must not be confounded with the affirmative particle "kû.")
pâk=throwing away of thing, abandonment, &c.
muin=means *with* when used *alone*(when used in conjunction with "shû" it denotes reflexive reciprocal action).

kü=ever, at one time or other, now and again, &c.
kümû=never.
tî=continuous action, generally.
gâ=used with root verb "gî"=go, to denote "gadding."
mô and vô=permissive ("mô" denotes a soliciting for permission to do anything, and "vô" a solicitation *to take with, go with, eat with*, &c., &c.)
gad=disinclination, generally.
bui=mix together.
lü=desiderative.
ling'a=ditto (seems to be an adjective used with root verbs).
kôm=covering up.
in=also a completive particle.
kû=affirmative particle.
gôr=celerity.
dân=ditto (this particle so far differs from the one immediately preceding it that while the first, "gôr," means *celerity*, "dân" means *at once, immediately*).
rû= } very, exceedingly.
lik= }
dîk=particle of vague probability.
buin=clearing.
tên=repair things, &c., &c.

A few examples showing how above are used—

Particle "mûr."

This particle is used chiefly with the *Perfect* Tense in "tô;" as—

bî-mûr-shû'tô...	I have given by mistake.
lû-mûr-shû'tô...	—— spoken ——
î-mûr shû'tô ...	—— done it ——
pâ-mûr-shû'tô...	—— struck ——
&c.	&c.

Nâ lâ-mûr-shû-â'mui'lô bilât* -kû-pui'a. You take mistake had if return again would.	If you had taken (it) by mistake you would have returned (it).
Î-mûr-shû-gê-ma'vô† Do mistake will no more.	I will not do it wrong again.

Particle "mân."

Also used *chiefly* with *Perfect* Tense, *with* or *without* shû; as—

bî-mân'tô.	I gave for fun.
lû-mân'tô.	I spoke.
î-mân'tô.	I did it.
&c.,	&c.

* Note use of "lât" and "kû" particle here.
† Ditto "vô."

Bî-mân*-dâk'kôm bî-mân* mâng'kôm Fun giving fun not giving ngâ bî-lât'-gê-kû-mâ"vô. I return again not.	Whether given in fun or not, I will not return it.
Na'ka â'gêr lât† î'mân yô'ka. You work with do play not.	Do not play with your work.

Particle "rik."

Ngâ buim da-lû'lâ rik-shû'tô. I him village in met not.	I met him in the village.
Dû-mai'ma lâm-bü'lâ gî-rik-shû yê'mui"lô Dumai to road on meet will if sim bî-lâng'kâ. this give.	If you meet Dumai on the road give him this.

Particle "âm vô."

"âm" may be, and often is, used *alone*, or in *conjunction* with "vô." If used in *conjunction* with "vô," the sense of completion is *intensified* to *its fullest*; as—

Nâ a-dî'lo nî-âm-yê'na ? You when washing will ?	When will you *finish* washing (clothes) ?
Â-gêr'em î-âm-tô'vô. Work finished have.	I have *entirely* finished the work.
Ngâ â-pông'em tü-âm-tô'vô. I liquor drink all have.	I have drunk *all* the liquor.

The completive particle "vô" (in its *stronger* form "vông") is, with the exceptions noticed later on, always tacked on to the *end* of the tense suffixes, *not*, as is the case with *nearly* all the other particles, placed *between* them and the root of the verb. "Vô" may be, and constantly is, used *alone*, as well as *with* other particles. It is the most *useful* and at the same time the most *plastic* particle the Miri language possesses, so much so that it is almost impossible to say *when*, or *where* it *cannot* be used. I give below a few examples:—

Long-ûm'kâ dû-vong. Days three is past.	It is three days ago.
Lâng-nyî'kâ kâ'vông. Year two gone by.	It is two years ago.
Ngâ olî-yâ'vông. I fell nearly.	I nearly fell.
Ngâ dâ-to'vô. I eat have finished.	I eat have finished. (Hind, "khâ chuka."
Ngâ gî-yê-pü'vô. Gî-yê'vô. Gî-pü'vô. Gî-len-pü'vô.	I will go, and on the point of moving. Do. do. move out or set out.

* "bî-dâkkôm"=giving "bî-mâng'kôm"=not giving.

† to work, lit., do work, is "âgîr îto-kâ."

Nâ ê'gü bî-lâ-mâ'vo-na"-yü? You again give able not more?	Can you give (me) no more.
Î-pü'num â-tî-kô'sin kâ'mâ vông. Do to anything at all exists not (now).	There is nothing more to be done.
Bui'ka sî*-nâm'a pô'lô pui†-keng'kâ vông. His dying moons six expired (have).	It is six months since he died.
Ngâ in-kâ'kâ lû-yê'na‡ mui-dû'vông. I what of speak shall I thinking. (*i.e.*, I have commenced thinking!)	I am thinking what to say.
Bui gî-lât-dâk-kû'vông. He return again has.	He has turned back.
Bui lâ'keng kî'shâ kâ'vô He finger like become.	He has become (through sickness as thin as) a finger.
Ngâ-lû'ka am'em kûm-shû'lâ ma-tôvô. We "dhan" granary in put have.	We have finished housing our dhan.

The cases where "vô" does *not* appear at the *end* of the tense suffixes are, (*a*) when it is used in conjunction with "dî," the particle of *vague probability*, (*b*) when used with the tenses of the *Subjunctive Mood*, (*c*) when used *interrogatively*; as—

Sê'kô dâ-âm'pô-yê"dî?§ Who eat finish first will?	Who will finish eating first.
Long kêng kâ-vô'dî. Days nine transpired probably.	Nine days may have transpired.
Sîlô sim î-vô'mui"lô gî'pü. This day this finish if go will.	If I finish this to-day, I will go.
Nâ dâ-tô-vô'yü? You eat have finished?	Have you finished eating?

Particle "po."

Nâ gî-pô'tô-kâ? You go first?	You go in front.
Ngâ î-pô'lâ gî'pü. I do first having go will.	I having done it will go.
Ngâ î-pông-gê'lâ gî'pü. I do first having go will.	I will do it ere I go.
Nâ dâ-pô-pui'â gî-pô-pui'â? You eat first go first?	Will you eat first or go first.

---

* Past participle of root verb "sî," with nominatival "a," showing that it is here used as a verbal noun.

† Numerical affix (*vide* page 40, *ante.*)

‡ Interrogative of verb.

§ Here we have no less than three distinct particles use together, *viz.*, "âm," "pô," and "dî."

Particle, "pui."

Sî pui-yê'dî pui-mâ-yê'dî? This suffice will suffice not will?	Will this suffice or not?
A! pui-yê'pü. Yes! suffice will.	Yes! it will suffice.
Nôm ai-mô'pü em'nâ bî'tô. You good (make) saying given to.	I gave (it) to do you good.
Bui'ka pui-nâm'kâ* âm-buin'em bî'to-kâ. His full rice give.	Give him a sufficiency of rice.
Ngâ'lû dâ-lû'lâ a-dî'lô pui-yê'na†? We village to when reach shall?	When shall we reach the village?
È-lûng'a‡ a-dî'lô puing-kâ'na†? Boat when arrive has?	When did the boat arrive?
Pôlô bû§-pui'dâk. Moon full is,	It is full moon.
Sî lâm'bü sî in-kâ'lâ pui-dû'na? This road this where reaches?	Where does this road lead?
Lông'a a-dit-kâ-vô'dî ngâ ken'mâ mui-pui-mâ'vô‖ Days how many elapsed I know not mind fill not.	I do not know how many days have elapsed,
È-lûng'a sâk'ka mô'teng a-dit'kâ pui-dû'na? Boat this from far how reaches?	How far can the boat go (up the river) from this?

Particle "lât."

This particle is used much in the same way as the Kachari verb "Fàfinnŭ" = to turn, *vide* page 27 of Revd. Mr. Endle's Kachari Grammar; "lât" used in conjunction with the root verbs, "gî" = *go*, "bôm" = *bring* or *carry*, "bê" = *give*, give us, to quote the Revd. Mr. Endle, such useful words as—

(Ngâ) gî-lât-kû'pü ... (I) will *come back*,
—— bôm-lât-kû'pü ... (I) will *bring back*.
—— bî-lât-kû'pü ... (I) will *give back*.
&c. &c.

Particle "pâk."

yôp-pâk'to-kâ ... throw away *things generally*.
pui-pâk'to-kâ ... ———— *water*.
ma-pâk'to-kâ ... *abandon anything* (mê=put or place).
(urling) gê-pâk'to-kâ ... throw *stone*.
stone
men-pâk'to-kâ ... drive out, or away.

---

* Numeral "kâ."
† Interrogative of verb.
‡ Nominatival "a."
§ "âbû" = whole, here "bûpui" = complete.
‖ "mui-pui-mâvô" = cannot.

Nâ âm-buin'em kâ-p'ilâ yôp-pâk- You rice why thrown to'yü? away have?	Why have you thrown away the rice?
Â-si'a* pui†-pâk'yô-kâ. Water throw away don't,	Do not throw away the water,
Sim kô sim yŭm-râ'lâ ma-pâk- This child this jungle in abandon yê'mui"lo si-yê'pü. will if die will.	If you abandon this child in the jungle, it will die.
Nôm ur-ling'em gê-pâk'-mô- You stones throw permit gê"mâ. will not.	I will not permit you to throw stones.

Particles "muin," "muin'shû."

"muin" used *alone* merely means *with*, and is used in *conjunction* with the particle "lå," when however "muin" is used in *conjunction with* "shû" (sort of reflective particle), it denotes *reflexive*, *reciprocal* action, and is equivalent to the Kachari "zlai;" as—

Bui ê-lû'lâ gi-muin'kâ, He boat with went.	He went *with* the boat.
Ngâ bui-ka'lâ i-muin'tô. I his (assistance with) did (it).	I did (it) *with* him (*i.e.*, with his assistance).
Ê-ki'a* gâm-pü'kü.‡ Dog bite will.	The dog will bite,
Ê'ki ki-ding'a* gâm-muin'shû"- The dogs bite one another pü'kü.‡ will.	The dogs will bite *one another*,
Nâ'lû kâ-pi'lâ gê-muin-shû- You why quarrelling with one another are? dû'na?	Why are you quarrelling with *one another*.

Particle "kû."

Ngâ bê-lâng'em dâ-kû'tô. I jack eaten have.	I have (at one time or other) eaten jack-fruit.
Ngâ bê-lâng'em dâ-kû'mâ. I jack eat never.	I never eat jack.
Nâ sit'em kâng-kû-tô'yü§? You elephant seen ever have?	Have you ever seen an elephant?

---

* Nominatival "a."

† "pui" means a pouring out.

‡ This is the affirmative particle "kû," softened to "kü" for the sake of euphony.

§ Interrogative of verb.

Gi-kâ-lâng-kû'kâ. Go away home.	Go away home.
Bi-lâttô-kâ'kû"kâ. Give back again.	Give (it) back again.
Lâ-len-tô-kû'kâ. Take out again.	Take it out again.
Nâ'lû a-di'lô â'reg lok'kâ gi-dâ-kû'na? You when fields from return?	When do you return from (your work in the) fields?

Particle "tî."

This particle is equivalent to the Kachari "bai;" as—

Pret-tâng'a* bêr'dûng. Bird flying is.	The bird is flying.
Pret-tâng'a* bêr-tî'dûng. Bird flying always is.	The bird is always flying about.
Bui â-pông'em tü-tî'dâ. He liquor drinking always.	He is always drinking liquor.
Nâ kâ-pi'lâ â-pông'em tü-tî-dû'na †? You why liquor drinking always?	Why are you always drinking liquor?

This particle "tî" may be, and often is, used in conjunction with the intensive particle "â;" as—

Bui â-pong'em tü-tî'â"dâ He liquor drinking everlastingly are.	He is everlastingly drinking liquor.
Nâ pân‡'em dâ-tî'â"dâ. You "pan" eating everlastingly are.	You are everlastingly eating "pan."

It is also often combined with the particles "muin" and "shû"; as—

Bû'lû §gê-tî-muin'-shû'-â"dâ. They quarrelling everlastingly are with one another.	They are everlastingly quarrelling with one another.

N.B.—The particle "â" is never used *alone.*

---

* Nominatival "a."

† Interrogative of verb.

‡ Assamese words.

§ Here we have no less than four particles (tî, muin, shû and â) clumped together, and this is not at all an uncommon practice.

Particle "gå."

This particle is not much used, and only in conjunction with the root verb "gî" = go; as—

Ngå ån-jå'kå gi-gå'pü. I little stroll will.	I will take a little stroll.

Particles "vô, mô."

Nå buim så dû-mô-pui'â*? You him here stay permit will?	Will you let him stay here?
Nå buim ngâ-ka'lâ dû-vô-pui'â*? You him my side to stay permit will.	Will you let him stay with me.
Buim nå-ka'lå gî-vô-lâng'kâ. Him your with go permit.	Bring him with you.
Bui'ka rôl'lâ gî'vô-kû-nâm"em â-mî'a kâ-tô'yü? His seizing carrying off persons see have.	Did any one see him seize and carry her off?

Particle "gad."

This is a very useful particle, and is constantly used. It is the *opposite* of the desiderative particle "lü"; as—

Ngå mâk'shâ† shâ-nâm'em kâng-gad'dûng. I dancing see disinclined am.	I am disinclined to see the dancing.
Dä-gad-dâk'kôm då-gad-mâng'kôm då'pü lâ-gî'dâ Eat disinclined being eat disinclined not being eat to must.	Whether inclined to eat or not, you must eat.

Particle "bui."

Yon-bui-shû'to-kâ=mix things.
Pui-bui-shû'to-kâ=mix liquids (pui=pour out).
Ma-bui-shû'to-kâ=place things together (ma=place a thing).

Examples.

Sim lâng dem lâng ma-bui-shû'yo-kâ. This and that and mix up do not.	Do not mix this and that (together).
Sim ân'yî sim lê-kô'pü ma-bui-shû'yô-kâ. These two these together mix up do not.	Do not place these two things together.

---

* Interrogative of verb.

† Mâkshâ shânâm=past participle of verb "mâkshâ shâ," with accusative case suffix "em."

Particles " ling'a, lü."

Examples showing use of "ling'a" have already been given. It ("ling'a") is more an adjective than anything else. The following examples will illustrate how "lü" is used:—

Ngâ â'si tü-lü'dûng I water drink wishing am.	I wish to drink [I (am) thirsty "tü-lingü."]

Particle "kôm."

This is a useful particle, though it has not a very extensive use: " tâk-kôm'to-kâ" apparently means to cover *a thing*, "pâ-kôm'to-kâ"=to close a road, to prevent people using same by mistake (pâ=cut jungle, &c.):—

Nâ'ka ming-mô'em gâ-sôr'lok Your face cloth with tâk-kôm-shû'yô-kâ. cover don't.	Do not cover your face with your cloth.
Á-pin'em tâk-kôm' to-ka. (Cooked) rice cover.	Cover up the rice.
A'la lâm'bü a'lem pâ-kôm'to-kâ. That there road that there close.	Shut that road there.
Ur'sing â-muing'kâ lâm-bü- Tree a road lâ ô-kom'dâ*. on fallen is.	A tree has fallen *across* the road.
Yâb'gô mô-kôm'to-kâ *or* si-kôm'to-kâ. Door close.	Shut the door.
Yâb-gô'a si-kôm-dû'vông. Door shut is.	The door is shut.

Particle " in."

There appears to be no real difference between this particle and "âm." They appear, in fact, to be interchangeable:—

Men-jâk'a si-in'kâng (*or* si-in-kâ'vô). Buffaloes dead all.	The buffaloes have *all* died.
Ngâ dâ-in'tô *or* dâ-in-tô'vô. I eaten all have	I have eaten *all*.

Particle "kû".

The use of this particle has already been illustrated so often that there is no occasion to give any more examples.

---

* " ô-kômdâ "=fallen, so as to cover up the road; " ô "=fall, " kôm "=particle alluded to above; " dâ " abbreviated form of substantive verb "âng."

Particle "gôr."

This particle is in constant use. It appears to be equivalent to the Kachari particle "lâng"; as—

Dûk'to-kâ=run.
Dûg*-gôr'to-kâ=run quickly.

Gî-âng-gôr-lâng'kâ. Come quickly.	Come quickly.
Gî-lât-gor'lâng-kû"kâ. Return quickly again.	Return (again) quickly.
É-lûng'em shân-gôr'to-kâ. Boat pole quickly.	Pole the boat quickly.
È-lûng'em dû-bôr'to-kâ. Boat paddle quickly.	Paddle the boat quickly.
Â-mî'em gôk-gôr'to-kâ. Man call quickly.	Call the man quickly.
Da'lâ sî-mon'a dûng, There deer is, âb-gôr'-lâng"kâ. fire quick.	There is a deer, fire quickly.

Particle "dân."

Ȧn-jâ-kâ'tê dû'yô-kâ, Little at all stay not, gî-dân'to-kâ. go at once.	Do not stay at all, (but) go *at once.*
Ngâ â-pin'em dâ-pô-dân'pü I rice eat first will immediately.	I will eat first, *immediately.*
Ê-lûng'em bôm-dân-lâng'kâ. Boat bring at once.	Bring the boat *at once.*
Gî-gôr-dân'to-kâ. Go quickly at once.	Go quickly, *at once.*

Particle "rû."

Ngôm bâ-tê-na† kâ bî'kâ. Me to large one give.	Give me a large one.
Ngôm bâ-tê'rû"-nakâ bî'ka. Me to large very one give.	Give me a very large one.
Â-sî'a bâ-tê-rûng'kâng. Water large very become has.	The river is (has become) very high.
Ai'dâk. Good is.	Good is.
Ai-rû'dâk. Good very is.	Good very is.
Â-mî'a bâ-jê'rûng"kâ gî-â'dûk. People many very come are.	Very many people have come.

* This "g" is merely euphonic.
† Adjectival "na."

Particle "lik."

It is difficult to say what this particle means *exactly*. It enters into the composition of a number of different words; as—

Lik-shû'to-kâ	Change a thing (clothes, or what not).
Pui-lik'to-kâ	Pour out water.
Pô-lik'to-kâ	Cover a human being.
Î-lik'to-kâ	Smear with oil, apply medicines outwardly.
Rî-lik'to-kâ	Destroy jungle, houses, &c., by fire.
Bî-lik'to kâ	Send a messenger.
Lû-lik'to-kâ	Send a letter or message.
Pur'lik	Upset a boat.
Kâ'lik	Pleased with.
Â'lik	Substitute.
Lâ'lik*	Reprisal.
Lik'to-kâ	Sow broadcast.
Gî-lik'to-kâ	Escort a person.

Particle "dî."

This particle, expressing vague probability, has often been illustrated in the Accidence.

Particle "buin."

Ur-buin'to-kâ	=	Wash (clean) rice, vegetables, plates, &c.
Tid-buin'to-kâ	=	Clean a thing by wiping.
Bur-buin'to-kâ	=	Clean pots and pans, &c., by scrubbing with sand, &c.
Pret-buin'to-kâ	=	Sweep clean (pret to-kâ=sweep).
Élûng âsl kâr-buin'to-kâ	=	Throw water out of a boat.
Dâ-buin'to-kâ	= }	Clean by eating (dâ=eat).
Yâk-buin'to-kâ	= }	Lick clean (yâk=lick).

These two last are used more as abuse than anything else. If A be the means of dirtying B's clothes or person, the latter may, in a rage, tell A to eat or lick it clean!

(*c*) Verbal tense suffixes may be put, generally, directly to (*a*) nouns, (*b*) adjectives; as—

(*a*) Examples.

Yŭm		Evening.
Yŭ'ma dûng	...	It is evening.
Yŭ'ma dûn'gai	...	It was evening.
Yŭ-ma'yê	...	It will eve.
Yu-ma'mui"lô	...	If it eves.
Yŭ-ma-mâng-a'-mui"lô	...	If it had not eved.
&c.,		&c.

*"lâ"=take, "lik"=change.

Ngâ-lû'ka ê'kum pui-dâ'dem Our house arriving whilst yŭ'ma dûn'gai. evening was.	It was evening when we reached home.
Mai-nâ'pü gi-kâ-lâng-kû'kâ yŭ- Quickly return ma'yê. evening will.	Return quickly. It will eve.

Kêmô=Dark.

Kê-mo'dûng ...	It is dark.
Kê-mô dûng'ai ...	It was dark.
Kê-mô'yê ...	It will (be) dark.
Kê-mô'mui"lô ...	If it is dark.
Kê-mô'kâng, Kê-mô-kâ'vô ...	It has become dark.
&c.,	&c.

Ai ê= Fruit.

A'la ur'sing a'la ai-ê-yê'pü. That (there) tree there fruit will.	That tree (there) will (bear) fruit.
Bâ-jê'pü ai-ê-yê'mui"lô âg-ling'a Much fruit will if boughs dîr-yê'pü. break will.	If it bears much fruit, the boughs will break.

(*b*) EXAMPLES.

Aia=Good, also well.

Ai'dâk ...	It is good.
Ai-dûn'gai Ai-dâg'ai	It was good.
Ai-yê'pü ...	It, will be good.
Ai-mui'lô ...	If (it) is good.
&c.,	&c.
Ê-ngâ'a* ai-dûng'ai ai-mâng- Fish good was good not â'mui"lê ngâ dâ-mâng'ai had been if I eat would not	The fish was good had it not been (so) I would not have eaten (it).
Ê-ngâ'a* ai-mui'lô rê'pü Fish good if buy will	If the fish is good, I will buy (it).
Sî â'din si ai'dâk yâ'mâng This meat this good is rotten not yâm'pô tê ai-yê 'pü. morrow also good will be.	This meat is good. It is not rotten. It will be good to-morrow also.

The same with "rû-bê'a"=*deaf*, "lê-vê'a"=*lame*, "mig-lû'a" =*blind*, "bâ-dâ'a"=*long*, *tall*, "tôr-nâm'a"=*strong*, &c., &c. In the last case, the tense suffixes would be attached to "tôr," the "nâ" being omitted.

16.—INTENSIVE PARTICLES.

The intensive particles appear to be "âm," "in," "tî," "â," "gôr," and "rû" (already noticed), inasmuch as they are used

---

* Nominatival "a".

in *addition* to the adjective, or adverb, whose sense they convey merely as a mode of *intensifying* the meaning required to be expressed, as—

EXAMPLES.

Âm â-puing'a* sân'kâng	The "dhan" has *all* withered.
"Dhan" all withered	

Here the adjective "â'puing'a" of *itself* sufficiently conveys the meaning *whole*, but the same may be intensified by adding "âm" to the root verb "sân"=*dry*, *wither*, in *addition* to "â-puing'a," as—

Âm â-puing'a* sân-âm'kâng	The *whole* (every bit) of the "dhan" withered.
"Dhan" all withered entirely.	

Again—

(1) Pô-dông'a* â-gin'pü o-ti-â'	It is *everlastingly* raining.
Rain always falling dâ. continuously.	
(2) Nâ â-gin'pü ni'tôm mô-ti-â'	You are *everlastingly* singing.
You always. dâ.	
(3) Ê'ek â-puing'a* si-in'kâng.	The pigs *all* died.
Pig all died (to an animal).	
(4) Si'tâ da ai-rû'pü bâ-tê rû'dâk	(The) elephant is exceedingly large.
Elephant it very large indeed is.	
(5) Ê-lûng'a mai-nâ'pü dû-gôr' tokâ.	Paddle the boat *quickly*.
Boat quickly paddle very.	

The last five examples might also be rendered by using the adjective or adverb *singly*.

As in Kachari, too, to again quote the Revd. Mr. Endle (*vide* page 30 of his Kachari Grammar), "in some few instances the noun is *repeated* in the verb when this latter stands in a specially close, almost technical, relation to the noun" as—

EXAMPLES.

Appui=egg.

Pô-rôk'a âp'pui pui'dûng.	The fowl is laying (eggs).
Fowl laying is.	

Dâmuir=a cloud.

Dâ'muir muir'dâk.	It is thundering.
Thundering is.	

---

* Adjectival *a*. Tacking the nominatival *a* unto the adjective "âpuing" is very common. I believe it is merely done for the sake of euphony.

There are a few more words which may be similarly treated.

17. Interrogative form of Verb.

The interrogative particles are, (*a*) "na," borrowed, one would think, from the Assamese,—with tenses other than the future in "pü;" (*b*) "â;" with the future in "pü;" (*c*) "yü;" as a connective, to mark, but often merely to imply, an alternative (it is equivalent, in fact, to the English conjunction *or*) with *all* tenses *save* the future in "pü" (probably on account of the hiatus which would occur); and (*d*), lastly, "lângâ," which is the *negative* interrogative; as—

(*a*) Examples.

Nâ in-kâ'kâ kô-dû'na ? You what seeking ?	What do you want ?
Ê-kûm'a in-kâ'lâ dû'na ? House where is ?	Where is the house ?
Nâ in'kôm î-dû'na ? You what doing are ?	What are you doing ?
Sim in'qua em-dû'na ? This what call ?	What (do you) call this ?
A'la in'qua ngôm-dû'na That (there) what noise is ?	What noise is that ?

(*b*) Examples.

Nâ ngôm bî-pui'â ? You me to give will ?	Will you give (it) to me ?
Nâ ngôm dâ-shûk-pui'â ? You me kiss will ?	Will you kiss me ?
Nâ ür-shû-kâ-pui'â ? You bathe purpose of (go) will ?	Will you go to bathe ?
Nâ sî'tem bôm-pui'â ? You elephant bring will ?	Will you bring the elephant ?

(*c*) Examples.

Â-sî'a â-rî-dû'yü ? Water deep is ?	Is the water deep ? (*or not* understood).
Mô'tê dû'yü â'nin dû'yü ? Far is near is ?	Is (it) far or near ? (*or not* understood).
Nâ tê'lâ dûng-ai'yü ? You there was ?	Were you there ? (*or not*).
Nâ â-pin'em dâ-tô'yü ? You food eaten have ?	Have you eaten ?
È'lû da â-kû-â'yü â-nû-â'yü ? Boat it old new ?	Is the boat old or new ?

(*d*) Examples.

Nâ gî-mâ-lâng'â ? You go not ?	Did you not go ?
Bui sî-pü-mâ-lâng'â ? He die will not ?	Will he not die ?

Bû'lû gi-gê-mâ-lâng'â ? They go will not ?	Will they not go ?
Nâ ni'tôm mô-lâ-mâ-lâng'â ? You sing able not? *	Can you not sing ?

Interrogative alternatives are formed by using the interrogative particle "na," in conjunction with the connective particle yü; as—

EXAMPLES.

Nâ buim pâ-tô-na'yü pâ-mâ-na'yü ? You him beat have beat not ?	Did you strike him or not ?
Nâ tü-tô-na'yü tü-mâ-na'yü ? You drink have drink not ?	Have you drank (it) or you ?
Nâ bi-tô-na'yü bi-mâ-na'yü ? You given have given not ?	Have you given (it) or not ?
Nâ buim pâ-yê-na'yü pâ-mâ-na'yü ? You him strike will strike not ?	Will you strike him or not ?
Nâ bi-yê-na'yü bi-ma-yê-na'yü ? You give will give not ?	Will you give (it) or not ?
Nâ gi-kâ-na'yü gi-mâ-na'yü ? You go have go not ?	Have you been or not ?
Bui i-dû-na'yü i-mâ-nay'ü ? He do is do not ?	Is he doing (it) or not ?
Bû'lû ni'tôm mô-dû-na'yü mô-mâ-na'yü? They singing are singing not?	Are they singing or not ?
Bui âm'em yik-dû-na'yü yik-mâ-na'yü? She?	Is she (?)
Nâ ê'gü bi-lâ-mâ-vô'na'yü ? You again give able not still ?	Can you give me no more ?

Interrogative *alternatives* are made with the future tense in "pü" as follows:—

EXAMPLES.

Nâ bi-pui'â bi-pü-mâng'â*? You give will give will not ?	Will you give (it) or not ?
Nâ i-pui'â i-pü-mâng'â ?* You do will do will not ?	Will you do (it) or not ?
Nâ tü-pui'â tü-pü-mâng'â ? You drink will drink will not ?	Will you drink (it) or not ?

"Di," the particle of *vague probability*, is also used sometimes as an *interrogative* particle, but *only* with "dû," (the *abbreviated* form of the substantive verb) and the future tense suffix "yê"; as—

EXAMPLES.

Á-rû'lâ kê-bûng'a dû'di ? Hole in mouse is ?	Is there a mouse in the hole (I wonder)?
Pô'dông ô-yê'di ? Rain fall will ?	Will it rain (I wonder)?

* "mâ" plus "â" with "ng" added to prevent hiatus.

18. Negative form of Verbs.

"mâ", and with some past tenses the *stronger* form "mâng" the negative particle signifying *not* either (*a*) immediately *follows* the root verb, (*b*) or it *follows* the tense suffix, (*c*) or it is placed *between* the root verb and the tense suffix; as—

(*a*) Examples.

Nâ â-tî'kô tê î'mâ. You anything at all do not.	You do not do anything.
Ê-kî'a rek'mâ. Dog bite not.	The dog does not bite.
Ngâ âm-buin'em bôm'mâ? I rice bring not.	I did not bring rice.
Ngâ gî'mâ. I go not.	I did not go.
É-kum'a dâ'dî ô'mâ. House leak not.	The house does not leak.
Ngâ buim pâ'mâ. I him strike not.	I did not strike him.

(*b*) Examples.

Ngâ buim kâ-tô'mâ. I him seen have not.	I have not seen him.
Ngâ bî-tô'mâ. I given have not.	I have not given (it).
Ngâ â-gôm'em lû-gê'*mâ. I words speak will not.	I will not speak.
Bui nôm pâ-gê'*mâ. He you strike will not.	He will not strike you.
Ngâ dâ-lâ'mâ. I eat able not.	I cannot eat.
Ngâ ü-mü'em pâr-lâ'mâ. I fire light able not.	I cannot light the fire.

(*c*) Examples.

Ngâ nî'tôm mô-mâng'ai. I singing not was.	I was not singing.
Ngâ ê-lû'lâ dû-mâng'ai. I boat in not was.	I was not in the boat.
Bui dâ-mâ'mui"lô. He eat not if.	If he does not eat.
Ngâ gî-mângâ'mui"lô. I go not had if.	If I had not gone.
Bui bî-mâ yê'mui"lô. He give not will if.	If he will not give.
Ngâ dâ-lâ-mâ-yê'mui"lö. I eat able not will if.	If I shall be unable to eat.

---

* *g* is, I believe, substituted for *y*, merely for the sake of euphony.

As already noticed, verbal tense suffixes may be attached *directly* to *adjectives*, *nouns*, *&c.*, and so in a similar manner may the negative particle "mâ"; as—

EXAMPLES.

Ngâ ki'mâ. I ill not.	I (am) not ill.
Bui lê-vê'mâ. He lame not.	He (is) not lame.
Ngâ ki-mang'ai. I ill not was.	I was not ill.
Sû-pâk kê-mô'mâ. Now dark not.	It (is) not dark now. &c., &c.

The *prohibitive* negative has already been noticed.

19.—ADVERBS.

The Adverbial suffix is "pü." The Adverb *proper* precedes the verb it qualifies, but if the adverbial sense is expressed, as it sometimes is, by a *particle only*, the latter is tacked on to the root verb, or to the tense suffix.

Adverbs may be classified as follows—

I.—OF TIME.

Si'lô=this day.
Yâm'pô=morrow.
Rô'ê=day after tomorrow.
Rôk'kê=day after that.
Ma'lô=yesterday.
Kôn'nô=day before yesterday.
Kông'kê=day before that.
Lô-dî'pü=daily.
Yüm-dî'pü=every evening.
Lê'kô lê'kô=sometimes.
A-dî-lô'dî=whenever.
Lê-kô'tê=once more.
Yâ'lâ=at night.
A-dak'ka=since when.
Da-lok'ka=since then.
Made by participle dâ'dem } =whilst.
Made by using completive particle "vô" or its stronger form "vông." } =ago, past.
Sû-pâk'pü=now.
Made by the particle of priority "pô" and sometimes by paraphrasing sentence. } =before, in point of time.
Made by particle "vô." } =after, subsequently in time.
A-gin'pü=always.
Rô-kôm'pü=early morning.
Rô-dî'pü=every morning.
Ngâk=late.
Si'lô mâ'lô=lately (lit., to-day, yesterday).
Sin'ying=this year.
Môn'ying=last year.
Lün'ying=next year.
Kôn'nô ma'lô. { =in bygone times (lit., day before yesterday and yesterday).
E'gü *or* lê-kô'tê=again.
Made by a particle "dâ" tacked on to present tense suffix of substantive verb. } = still, yet.

A-dî'lô sin mâ=never (lit., when even not).
Da-lô'pü=then.
Made by particle "kî'râm."} =almost.
Made by particle "yâ" in combination with "vô."} =nearly.

II.—Of Place.

Sâ'pü=here.
Â-pui'lâ=everywhere.
A'lâ=there, near and in sight.
Tê'lâ=there, upstream.
Ba'lâ=there, downstream.
A-lok'ka=thence.
A-nin'pü=near.
Lê-kô'pü=together.
Lin'gin=upstream.
Sok'ko=downstream.
Tâ-la'lâ=above.
Kê-êg'lâ=below.

III.—Of Quantity.

Sî-dî'kâ=this much.
A-dî'kâ=that „
Made by particles "pü" and "di"} =about.
Lê-kô'tê=more.
Ai-rû'pü=very, exceedingly.
Sin, tê=also.
Made by a particle "â".} =only.

IV.—Of Quality.

Kâ-shû'lâ= {carefully (lit., seeing self).
Ai-mâ'pü=badly.
Deng-um'pü=slowly.
Ai'pü=well.
Made by particle "yâ."} =almost.
Ê'song=perhaps.
Bê-rôk'pü=certainly.
Dê-pî'lâ=therefore.
Mai-nâ'pü=quickly.
Sim'pü=in this way.
Da'pü=in that way.

V.—Interrogative.

Kâ-pî'lâ=why?
In-ka'lâ=where?
A-dî'lô=when?
In-ka-lok'ka=whence.
Kâ'pü= {how (in what manner, by what means).
A-dit'kâ = {how many, how much, how often.

It may be as well to illustrate a few of the above, especially the manner in which the *interrogative* and *relative* adverbs are used:—

Examples illustrating the manner in which some of the adverbs given above are used.

Ngâ lô-dî'pü ür-shû'dâ.
I daily bathe.
} I bathe *daily*.

Ngâ lô-dî'pü rô-kôm'pü ü-mü'em pâr'dâ.
I daily early morning fire light.
or
Ngâ rô-dî'pü ü-mü'em pâr'dâ.
I early morning every fire light.
} I light the fire *every morning early*.

Lê'kô lê'kô ngâ ê-ngâ'em gâg'dâ.
Sometimes I fish catch.
} *Sometimes* I catch fish.

Lê kô'tê nî'tôm mô'tokâ.
Once (or again) also sing.
} Sing *once more*.

Ngôm lê-kô'tê bi'kâ. Me to more give.	Give me *some* more.
Tâng-nyi'kâ vông, *or* tâng-nyi-a'vông. Two years ago, years two ago.	Two years *ago*.
Si'lô lô-nyi'-avông buim kâ-nâm'a. This day days two ago him seen.	I saw him two days *ago*.
Ngâ'ka gi-rô'sim bui gi-âng-kâ'yü ? My going after he came has?	Did he come *after* my departure.
Ngâ'ka gi-rô'sim nâ in'kôm i-tô'na? My departure you what do have?	What did you do *after* my departure.
Bui'ka gi-â-mâng-â'dâ pü ngâ gi'pü. His coming not still to I go will.	I will go *before* he comes. (His coming not to I go will.)
Pô'dông ô-mâng-â-dâ'pü bui gi'kâ. Rain fallen not yet to he gone had.	He went *before* the rain came.
Si'lô* ma'lô ai-rû'pü âng-ki'rê. Lately very warm.	It (has been) *very* warm lately.
Kôn'nô† ma'lô ngâ-lû'ka dâ-lûng'a Pâ'dâm â'di â-nin'lâ dûn'gai. In bygone times our village Abor hills near to was.	In *bygone times* our village was close to the Abor hills.
Tûr-dûng-â'dâ. Alive is yet.	(It) *yet* lives.
Pui-â dûng-â'dâ. Light is still.	(It) is *still* (day) light.
Tûr-dûng-â-dâ'yü ? Alive is still?	Is (it) *still* alive ?
Ngâ yüp-pü'dâ. I sleep will still.	I will *still* sleep (*i.e.*, I will sleep more).
Ngâ dâ-pü'dâ. I eat will still.	I will *still* eat (*i.e.*, I will continue eating).
Ngâ ân-jâkâ dû-pü'dâ. I little stay will still.	I will stay a *little longer*, *i.e.*, I will *yet* remain.

Simple *negation* with this adverb (*still*) is formed by substituting the negative particle "mâ" *or* "mâng," for "dûng;" as—

EXAMPLES.

Bui gi-mâ'dâ *or* gi-mâng-â'dâ. He come not yet.	He has *not yet* come.
Ngâ'lû âm'ém gât-mâng-â'dâ. We *dhan* cut not yet.	We have *not yet* cut our *dhan*.
Dâ'nyi wâng-mâ'dâ. Sunset not yet.	It is *not yet* sunset.

The particles "yâ" and "kirâm" appear to be interchangeable—

Ngâ ô-lê-yâ'vô. I fell nearly.	I *nearly* fell.

* "Silô malô"=lit., this day, yesterday.
† "Kônnô malô"=lit., day *before* yesterday, yesterday.

Ngâ yü yâ'vông. I slept nearly.	I *nearly* slept.
Bui sî-kî'râm tûr-kî'râm dûng. He dead almost alive almost is.	He is almost dead.

(Freely translated, I fancy it means between the two.)

Â'gêr î-âm-kî'râm-dûvông. Work finished almost is.	The work is nearly all finished.
Â'gêr î-âm-kî'râm'tô. Work finished almost have.	I have almost finished the work.
Gâ-sôr'a pû-tîr-kî'râm-dû'vô. Cloth dry almost is.	The cloth is almost dry.
Â-lâk'em ü'mü ûg-kî râm'tô Hand fire burnt almost.	I (have) almost burnt my hand.

"Lê-kôpü," = *together*, requires illustrating, inasmuch as it is usually used with a verbal particle, "bâ'shû," *peculiarly its own*; as—

EXAMPLES.

Ngâ'lû lê-kô'pü dû-bâ-shû'tô. We together sat.	We sat together.
Ngâ'lû lê-kô'pü ê-lûng'em pâ-bâ-shû'tô. We together boat cut.	We cut the boat together.
Ngâ'lû lê-kô'pü nîtôm mô-bâ-shû'lâ"jê. We together sing let's.	Let us sing together.
Nâ'lû le-kô'pü mâk'shâ shâ-bâ-shû'yô-kâ. You together dance not.	Do not dance together.

"Lê-kôpü" is often *dispensed* with, and the sense of *together* rendered by "ba'shû" *alone*; as—

Bûn'yî ê-lûng'em pâ-bâ-shû'tô. Those two boat cut together.	These two cut the boat together.

or

Nâ'lû lâng ngâ'lû kâ-râm-bâ-shû'pü. You and we enemies together will (be).	We shall be at enmity (together).

"Kônnô malô" may be used to express *any* length of *expired* time (from a month to ten years) according to the emphasis put upon the "lô" in "mâlô," and the length of the *pause* made before it is pronounced

Sû'pâk â'mô â-pui'lâ â-sî'a, Now earth everywhere water, dûng dî-gin'lâ in-kâ-lâ'tê â-sî'a is cold weather in anywhere at all water kâ mâng. exists not.	There is water *everywhere* now, (but) in the cold weather you will find water nowhere.
A'la â-dî'a ai-rû'pü ô-it'dâk. That there mountain very high is	That (there) mountain is a *very* high one.
Sî ai-rû'pü tî'dâk This very sweet is	This is *very* sweet.
Sî gâ'sôr sî ai-rû'pü bet'kâng. This cloth this very torn.	This cloth is *much* torn.

E-lûng'a bâ-dâ'dâk sin bôr-tê'dâk sin Boat long is also wide is also.	The boat is long (and) *also* wide.
Ngôm lê kô'tê *or* ân-jâ-kâ'tê bi'kâ. Me to again also little also give.	Give me some *more*.

More is sometimes made as follows :—

Dem pü'num bâ-jê âng'kâ mui'dûng. That than much desire.	I want *more* than that.
Nâ ê'gû bi-lâ-ma'vôna"yû ? You again give able not more ?	Can you give me no *more* ?
Ngâ dû tâk'kâ pü'dî sâ yê'pü I year one about have reside will	I shall reside here *about* a year.
Ngâ â'mî ê-ing'kâ pü'dî kâ'tô. I men ten about saw.	I saw *about* ten men.
Kâ-shû'lâ gi lâng'kâ lâm'bü bê-lâb'a. Seeing go road slippery.	Go *carefully*, the road is slippery.
Sim'pü î'to-kâ. This wise do (it).	Do it *this wise*.
Da'pü î'to-kâ. That wise do (it).	Do it *thus*.
Bui kâ'pü î'tôn ? He how do has.	*How* did he do it?
Nâ kâ-pi'lâ î-tô'na ? You why do have ?	Why did you do (it).
Bû'lû a-di'lô î-tô'na ? They when do have ?	When did they do (it) ?
Bui a-di'lô î-tô'dî ngâ ken'mâ He when do have I know not	I don't know when he did (it).
Bui kâ-pi'lâ î-tô-na'dî ngâ ken'mâ. He why do have I know not.	I don't know why he did (it).
Bui kâ'pü î-tô'dî ngâ ken mâ. He how do have I know not.	I don't know how he did (it).
Nâ in kâ'lâ î-tô'na ? You where do have ?	Where did you do (it) ?
Nâ in-kâ'lâ î-yê'na ? You where do will ?	Where will you do (it).
Bui in-kâ'lâ î tônâ'dî ngâ ken mâ. He where do have I know not.	I don't know where he did (it).
Bui in-kâ'lâ î-yê-na'dî ngâ ken mâ. He where do shall I know not.	I don't know where he will do (it).
Nâ in-ka-lok'ka gi-â-dâng'na ? You where from come have ?	Whence did you come ?

20.—PREPOSITIONS,—IN MIRI POSTPOSITIONS.

Â'nin=near.
In-gem'lâ=without.
Tâ-lê'lâ=upon.
Râ-dâ'lâ=among.
Â-râ'lâ=within.
Kê-êg'lâ=in the middle, between.

The (English) prepositions *with*, *from*, *in* or *into*, *to* or *unto*, *for*, *before*, &c., are made by using *particles*; as—

EXAMPLES.

Ngâ'ka â-nin'lâ gi-â-lâng'kâ My (side) near to come.	Come *near* (to) me.
In-gem'lâ ma'to-kâ. Outside put.	Put (it) *outside*.
Si'tâ tâ-lê'lâ ma'tô-kâ. Elephant upon put.	Put (it) *upon* the elephant.
Ngâ'ka men-jâk'a âng-ü'na My buffalo others men'jâk râ-dâ'lâ dûng. buffaloes among is.	My buffalo is *among* the others.
Kê-bûng'a â'rûng â-râ'lâ Mouse hole inside dûng. is.	The mouse is *inside* the hole.
Kô-pâk'a tâ'sê kê-êg'lâ Plantains straw between ma'to-kâ. put.	Put the plantains *between* straw.

The mode of rendering sentences in Miri in which in English the prepositions *with*, *from*, *in*, and *to* have been already frequently illustrated:—

Si nâ'ka pü. This you of to.	This is *for* you.
Nâk'em pü'nâm bat-tê-yâ'dâ. Yours than larger.	It is too large *for* you.
Ngâ'ka kê-râ'sâ (front here) *or* kê-râ'lâ (front in) dâk'to-kâ. My front here *or* front in stand.	Stand *before* (in front of) me.
Ngâ bui'ka kâng-kâ'lâ buim pâ'tô. I his sight in him struck.	I struck him in his *presence*.

21.—CONJUNCTIONS.

Dê-pi'lâ=therefore.
Lâng=and.
Sin, tê=neither, nor, also, too
Mui'lô=if (when).

The following examples will illustrate how the above are used, as also the manner in which the remaining conjunctions are formed in Miri:—

Bâ'jê pô'dông ô'kâ dê-pi'lâ Much rain fell therefore lâm-bü'a* bê-lâb'dâk. road slippery is.	Much rain fell, *therefore* the road is slippery.

Nâ'ka â-jon'a lâng ân'gü Your companion and other mî'-ûm'ma ân-jâ'kâ bîlâng'kâ. girl to little give.	Give your companion *and* the other girl some.
Nâ lâng ngâ'a* yâm'pô You and I morrow tê'lâ tôk-kût†'pü there go down stream will.	You *and* I will go down the river to-morrow.
Nâ'nä bui lâng bâ'bû bui Mother she and father he lû-muin-shû'dâ. quarrel with one another.	(The) mother *and* father quarrel with one another.
Bui lâng ngâ kâ-râm-bâ‡-shû- He and I enemies dûng. are.	He *and* I are enemies.
Âng'kîr sin mâ ân'chî sin mâ. Hot also not cold also not.	It is *neither* hot not cold.
Da â'mî da âgom'em That man that words tê lû-lâ'mâ yê-rûng'a even speak able not ears tê tâl-lâ'mâ. also hear able not.	That man (there) can *neither* speak nor hear.
Ngâ sin gî'pü. I also go will.	I *also* will go.
Ngâ tê mâk'shâ shâ-lâ' pü. I also dance able am.	I *also* can dance.
A-pông'a kû-mui'lô ngâ Liquor sour if I tüng-gê'mâ. drink will not.	*If* the liquor is sour, I will not drink (it).
Ngâ lû-to'mui"lô bui I say have if he ken-yê'pü. know will.	*If* I have said (it), he will know.

The conjunction *either* is made by the use of "mui'lô," which includes the correlative, *or*; as—

Bui mâ mui'lô nâ mai'nâm He not if you false â-gôm'em lü'tô. words spoken have.	*Either* he *or* you have spoken a falsehood.
Nâ yôg-mô-mâ' mui"lô You lose make not if lur-shû-tô-na'pü ? hide have po sibly ?	You have *either* lost *or* possibly hidden it.

* Nominatival "a."

† Tôk to-kâ=go downstream by boat; gî-tôk to-kâ=ditto by land.

‡ *Vide ante*, where use of this particle is explained.

The (English) conjunction *or* is generally made by the interrogative particle "yü," which is then tacked on to the interrogative particle "na". In some cases, however, such as when the future tense in "pü" is used, or when "dî," the particle of vague probability, is used in conjunction with the future tense suffix "yê," interrogative alternatives, or alternatives expressive of *doubt* are placed together *without* any disjunctive conjunction as—

Nâ gî-pni'â gî-pü-mâng'â? You go will go will not?	Will you go *or* not?
Nâ buim pâ-tô-na'yü pâ-mâ-na'yü You him strike have strike not	Did you strike him *or* not?
Tem-pü-log'yü gî-yê'na ê-lû-log'yü Land by go shall boat by gî-yê'na? go shall?	Shall we go by land *or* by boat?
Sim â'pông sim tü-lâ-yê'dî This liquor this drinkable will tü-lâ-mâ-yê' di? drinkable not will?	Shall I be able to drink this liquor *or* not?

The (English) conjunction *although* is made by using the present participles; as—

Gî-â-lâng'kâ em-tô' gôm bui Come saying have he gî-â'mâ. come not.	*Although* I told him to come, he came not.
Dûm'pû dâk'kôm ngâ mû'jî Grey notwithstanding I old (man) (lit being,) mâ. not.	*Although* I am grey, I am not old.
Buim pâ-dâk'kôm kâb mâ. Him striking cry not.	*Although* I beat him, he did not cry.
Ngâ'ka â-kî'a kî-dâk'kôm â-pin'em My stomach aching food dâ-lâ'pü. eat able am.	*Although* my stomach aches, I can eat.

Illustrations of the Miri equivalent for *than* have already been given.

Ditto ditto *because.*

Until is made as follows—

Mâk'shâ shâng-âm'mâ tâ-kâm'em Dancing finished not whole (time) dû'pü. stay will.	I will remain *until* the dancing is over.

Nî'tôm mô-âm'mâ tâ-kâm'em Singing finished not whole (time) dû'pü. stay will.	I will stay *until* the singing is finished.
Nâ'ka gî-âng-kû'mâ tâ-kâm'em Your arrival not whole (time) dû'pü. stay will.	I will remain *until* you arrive.
Pô-lôk'a sî'mâ tâ-kâm'em Moon die not whole (time) dû'pü. stay will.	I will remain *until* this moon expires.
Kê-mô'mâ tâ-kâm'em ngâ Dark not whole (time) I dâ-lû'lâ dû'tô. village in stayed.	I stayed in the village *until* it was dark.

As far as is made as follows—

EXAMPLES.

Ngâ'ka â'sî sî'nâm tâ'kâm My water gone whole (distance) da â-tê-dûng'ai. it shallow was.	*As far as* I went the river was fordable.
Ngâ'ka gî'nâm tâ'kâm da My gone whole (distance) it lâm'bü ai-dûng'ai. road good was.	*As far as* I went the road was good.

Compound words.

The Miri language abounds in compound words, but I do not pretend to be able to systematically *classify* them. The following are a *few* of those in *general* use—

Â'jon=companion (â=come, enter, &c.)
Gi'jon*=road companion (gî=a moving, going).
Yûp'jon=sleeping companion (yûp=sleep).
Ki'jon=sick companion (kî=sick).

† { Am lik-dî'ü=dhan sowing *time* (âm=paddy, lik=sow broadcast).
Shum-dî'ü=weaving *time* (shûm=weave).
Yûp-dî'ü=sleeping time (yûp=sleep).
Gî-dî'ü=going time (gî=go). }
&c. &c.

Dâ'mui... { accompaniment to rice, such as salt, vegetables, meat, &c., &c., dâ=eat, mui=probably desire).
Dâ'kô=eating place (dâ=eat).
Yûp'kô=sleeping place (yûp=sleep).

---

* *Vide post*, where there is a sentence illustrating use of this word.

† These are all used as adjectives.

Gi'kô*=going place (gî=go).
Shûm'kô=weaving= (shûm=weave).
Ûm'ü pâr'kô=fire (ümü pâr=light fire).
Ma'kô=place to put things (ma=put, or place, a thing).
Á'si pui-pâk'kô=place to throw away water (Âsi=water, puipâk, throw away water).
Tâ'kir shûk'kô=place to spit (tâkir shûko=spit).
&c., &c.
Bûk'pem=double-barrel gun (âbûk=gun).
Ô'pem=twins (ô=birth).
Rôd'bâk=rubber-tree juice (rônna=rubber-tree).
A'bâk= tree juice generally.
Pui'môr=yoke of egg (âpui=egg. No word for white of egg except â'sik=skin).
Tân-yi'ra=laughable to hear (tâ=hear, yir=laugh).
Kâng-yi'ra=laughable to see, kâ=see, yir=laugh).
Nâm-kê'a=smell of urine (nâm=smell).
Nâm-shûn'ga=smell of excrement, rotten fish, &c.
Nâm-di'ga=anything stinging nose, as chillies, &c. (nâm=smell, dig=sting, smart).
Nâm-mun'ga=burnt smell.
Nâm-kô-sân'ga=bitter smell (nâm=smell, kô-sângü=bitter).
Nâm-yin'ga=smell of herbs, &c.
Nâm-kû'a=sour smell (nâm=smell, kû=sour).
Mûr'kông kân'nâ=wealthy (lit., murkông=rupees kânnâ=possessed of).
Mûr'kông kâ-mâ'nâ=poor.
Ngâ sân=dried fish (ê ngâ=fish.)
Din san=dried meat (âdin=meat.)

Compound verbs have already been noticed.

Shortening of words.

Perhaps the most curious, as also most noticeable feature of the language is the facility with which syllables of a word are *rejected*, either because the true root of the word is independent of them, or simply because the genius of the language tends to *abbreviation*, for instance:—

"Shû" is the root of the verb to *wash*; compound this with "lâk'po"=*hand*, and the latter drops its *last* syllable and appears as "lâ'shûk;" as—

Ngâ lâ-shûk†-shû'pü. I hands wash will.	} I will wash my hands.

* This word is often heard; as ngâka gîkô kâ mâ=I have no place (in particular, to visit).

† This *k* is merely euphonic, and the second "shû" is the reflective particle.

Again, "â'muir"=*body*, when combined with "shû" appears as "ür'shû;" as—

Ngâ ür-shû-kâ'pü. I bathe purpose of will (go).	I will go and bathe.

Take again "kî"=*count*, *measure*: "bôm'yâm"=*fathom*, in composition with it becomes "yâm;" "lâg'du"=*cubit*, becomes "dûk;" "pin gôp"=*span*, becomes "gôp;" as—

E-lûngem yâm-kî'tokâ Boat fathom.	Fathom the boat.
Dî-bângem dûk-kî'tokâ Bamboo cubit.	Cubit the bamboo.
U-kâ'em gôp-ki'tokâ. Stick span.	Span the stick.

Similarly, *certain* words in *combination* with *numerals* lose their *first* syllable, as already noticed.

A few more words are given in their *shortened* state elsewhere, but it may be as well to reproduce them here. They are—

Bûk'pem=double-barrel gun ("â'bûk"=gun).
O'pem=twins.
Rôd'bâk=rubber ("ronnü ursing"=rubber-tree; in this instance it is the last syllable dispensed with).
Pui'môr=yellow of egg ("â'pui"=egg).
Ngâ sân=dry fish ("ên'gâ"=fish).
Din sân=dry meat (â'din=meat).
Mîg'yâp=a wink (of the eye) ("â'mîk"=eye, "yâp"=flap or move about).
Og'yâp=beckon a person.
A'kâp kâp'to-kâ=roof a house ("âkâp"=roof).
A'min min'to-kâ=to name ("âmin"=name).
A'sî sîto-kâ=wade ("âsî"=water).
Sî'pût=froth from water ("â'sî"=water.)
*A'pût= ditto liquor ("â'pong"=liquor).
Pin'pût= ditto rice while being cooked ("â'pin"=cooked rice).

Then we have "ânyûk"=breast, "nyûkpî"=nipple of breast.

PART III.—SYNTAX.

Having enumerated a few of the most common rules applicable to the syntactical part of the Miri language, I shall follow the plan adopted by the Revd. Mr. Endle in his Kachari grammar, *viz.*, instead of attempting, with my present limited knowledge of the language, to lay down a complete sketch of

* One would think this ought to be "pongpût."

the Syntax of the Miri language, I shall, in addition to those already given in the Accidence, "give a number of typical and illustrative sentences arranged in groups, following the order of the different parts of speech, and numbered with reference to the sections bearing the same numbers in the Accidence, which will, it is hoped, serve to show the changes and modifications undergone by the different parts of speech when brought into syntactical relation with each other."

1. The order of words in a predicative sentence are, (1) subject, (2) direct object, (3) indirect object, (4) verb.

2. In an interrogative sentence the order is (1) subject, (2) indirect object, (3) direct object, (4) verb.

3. The adjective can either precede or follow its noun.

4. The adverb precedes the verb, or adjective that it qualifies.

I.—NOUNS.

1. Gender.

Mû'jî da kî'dâk. Old man he ill is.	*The old man* is ill.
Ur'jâ da lê-vê'dâk. Old woman she lame is.	The *old woman* is lame.
Ngâ-lû'ka miûm â-puing'a mâk'shâ shâng ken'mâ. Our young women all dancing know not.	All our *young women* (girls) cannot dance.
Yâ'mê kî'dî tê â'kô â'kô mâk'shâ shâng ken'dâ. Young men too some dancing know.	Some *young men* can also dance.
Ngâ'ka ô'ma â-ûm'kâ an'a â-nyî'kâ dûng. My daughters three sons two are.	I have three *daughters* and two *sons*.
Sî kô mil'vô sî ai'mâ This boy this good not.	This is a bad *boy*.
Sî-ta'a* ta-bâ-kâ'dî ?† Elephant male one is ?	Is it a *male* elephant ?
Er-bâ'a* lâng *er-na'a dûng. Pigs male and pigs female are.	There are swine, *male* and *female*.
Nâ-lû'ka pô'rôk rôk'pô *kî-ding'a yâ'lâ kôk'dûng. Your fowls male night in crow.	Your (village) *cocks* crow in the night.

* Nominatival *a*.

† Particle of vague probability.

Ngâ'ka â'pui pui'na* pô-rôk'a† â-ûm'kâ My egg egg laying fowls three dûng. are.	I have three laying *hens*.
A'da ur'sâ ki'dî da a-dit'kâ sâ'bâ Those mithon those how many males dû'dî‡ sâ'na a-dit'ka du'di?‡ are females how many are?	How many of those "mithon" are *males* and how many *females*.
A'la e'ek er'na a'la ê-ing'kâ an'a dûng. That (there) sow that ten young is.	That *sow* has ten young ones.
Nâ-lû'ka ê'ek er'bâ er'nem kâ-pi'lâ You pigs male female why tûm-mâ'na? shut up not?	Why don't you keep your pigs, *males* and *females*, shut up.

2. *Number.*

Â'mî ki'dî da âp-kâ'pü gi'kâ. The men they shoot purpose of gone.	The *men* have gone to shoot.
Â-mi'a si-yê'vông,§ *or* si-kân‖-dû'vông. Man die will die	The *man* is dying.
Mî'ma kî-ding'a ri'gû mô'dûng. Women weeding are.	The *women* are weeding.
Sim-yâ'a si-mon'em dâ'dâ. Tiger deer eat.	*Tigers* eat deer.
Ê-ki'a râ'dûng. Dog barking is.	The *dog* is barking.
Ê-ki kiding'a gâm-muin-shû'dûng. Dogs biting one another are.	The *dogs* are fighting together.
Sî gâ'sôr ki-ding'a koi-â'dâk. These clothes dirty are.	*These* clothes are dirty.

3. *Case.*

Ê-kum'a mô'tê dû'yü â'nin dû'yü? House far is near is?	Is the *house* far or near?
Nâ'ka gâ-lû'ka â-muir'lâ pui'mâ. Your jacket body to reaches not.	Your *jacket* does not fit.
A'mî ki-ding'a gi-â'dâk. Men come are.	The *men* are come.
Bui'kâ me-ang'a ki'dûng. His wife ill is.	His *wife* is ill.
Nâ'ka dûm-wit'em tûp-shû'to-kâ. Your hair comb.	Comb your *hair*.
Ngâ ê-lûng'em ai'pü rin'tô. I boat well tie (fasten) have.	I have fastened the *boat* well.

* Adjectival *na*.
† Nominatival *a*.
‡ Particle of vague probability.
§ Lit., will commence dying.
‖ Lit., is commencing to die.

Nâ'ka êg'em lik-shû'to-kâ. Your petticoat change.	Change your *petticoat* (Assam. meklâ).
Nâ â-pin'em dâ-tô'yü ? You rice eaten have?	Have you eaten (your) *rice*.
Ü-mü'em pâr'to-kâ. Fire light.	Light the *fire*.
Ngâ'ka ô'ma ka'pü rê'tô. My daughter for bought.	(I) bought (it) for my daughter.
Bû'lûm â-pông'em bî'tô. Them to liquor given have.	I gave them *liquor*.
Ngôm lâm-bü'em len-kân-lâng'kâ. Me to road show.	Show me the *road*.
Sim nâ'ka buir-ma'em bî'to-kâ. This your brother to give.	Give this to your *brother*.
Nâ'ka â-bûk'em Dû-mai'ma bî'tô Your gun Dumai to given have.	I have given your gun *to Dumai*.
A-lok'ka ur'sing â'muing a-lok'ka That there from tree that there from ân'na â-puing'a ô-lek-âm'kâng. leaves all fallen.	All the leaves have fallen from that tree there.
Sâk kô sâk yôk-shi'kem This from child this from knife lâ-tô-kû'kâ. take back.	Take back the knife from this child.
Men-jâk'lok oi'to-kâ. Buffalo from descend.	Get off the buffalo.
Nâ'lû ê-ngâ'em ur-sâp'lok gâg-dû'yü ? You fish net with catch do ?	Do you catch fish with a net ?
Pret'tâng bêr-dâ'dem (*or* bêr-dû'em) ngâ Birds flying whilst I â-bûk'lok âb-lâ'pü. gun with shoot able.	I can shoot birds flying with a gun.
Nâ'lû gâ'sôr shûm'nâm shü-pâk'em You cloths woven cotton in-kâ'lok pâ-dû'na ? where from get ?	Where do you get the cotton for weaving your cloths from ?
Â'si tâ-lêlâ pû-lem'lâ gi'dâ. Water surface on floating goes.	(It) floats *upon* the water.
Â-si'lâ yôp-pâk'to-kâ. Water into throw.	Throw it *into* the water.
Râ-dâ'lâ ma'to-kâ. Centre in place.	Place it *in* the middle.
Bui'ka ê-kum'a â-nin'lâ dûng. His house near to is.	His house is near.
Sâ ur'sing ôg'yüm sâ dû'to-kâ. Here tree shade here sit.	Sit here (in the) shade (of the) tree.

4.—ADJECTIVES.

Da-mui'lô bui ai-mâ'na â-mi'a. That if he good not man.	If so, he is a bad man.

Tôr′na â-sî′a. Strong water.	Strong, or swift, water.
Bà-dâ′na ê-lûng′kâ. Long boat.	A long boat.
Ân-da′na û-kâ′kâ. Short stick.	A short stick.
Ân-jâ′na ân-na′kâ. Small leaf.	A small leaf.
Da â′mî da bâ-dâ′dâk. That man that tall is.	That man is tall.
Si′ta tôr-nâm′a. Elephant strong.	The elephant is strong.
U-mü′a gû-nam′a. Fire hot.	The fire is hot.
Ai-rû′pü ân-ching′û. Very cold.	It is very cold.
Yôk′shik da ai-rû′pü râd′dâk. Knife it very sharp is.	The knife is very sharp.

Comparison.

Sî mî′ma si ngâ′ka â-bui-yâ′na buir′ma. This female this my elder sister.	This is my elder sister.
A′dem pü′num sî bâ-tê-yâ′dâk. That than this larger is.	This is larger than that.
Ngâ′ka buir′ma â-mê-yâ′na â-nyî′ka dûng. My sisters younger two are.	I have two younger sisters.
Môn′yingâ-pui-lok′em pü′num bâ-jê-yâ′na rôd-bâk′em se′kô pâ-tô′na? Last year all from than more rubber who cut?	Who cut the most rubber of all last year?
Kâm′tî mât-shik′em pü′num Pâ′dâm mât-shik′a ai-yâ-dû′yü ai-yâ-dû′yü? Khampti daos than Abor daos better are?	Are the Abor daos better than the Khampti ones?
Kâm′tî mât-shi′ka â-pui-lok′em pü′num ai-yâ′dâk. Khampti daos all from than better are.	The Khampti daos are the best of all.
Î î-pûk′em pü′num a-bûk′a ai-yâ′dâ. Bow arrows than gun better is.	A gun is better than a bow and arrows.
Mî′pak bê-lâng′em pü′num Pâ′dâm bê-lâng′a ai-yâ′dâk. Assamese jack than Abor jack better is.	Abor jack is better than Assamese jack.

Ngôm pü'num nâ'ka â bâ-tê-yâ'dâk. Me than your heart larger is.	You are more courageous than I.
Ngôm pü'num bui dûg-bân-yâ'dâ. Me than he run faster does.	He runs faster than I do.

6.—Numerical Adjectives.

Mi'shing ê-ing'kâ ê-ngâ'em gâg'dûng. Miris ten fish catching are.	Ten Miris are catching fish.
Â'mî ê'ing â-pî'kâ lâm-bu'em pâ'dâng. Mem ten four (*i.e.*, forty) road cutting are.	Forty men are cutting jungle on the road.
Ê'ek dôr-keng'kâ si'kâng. Pigs six died.	Six pigs died.
Pô'rôk pîr-pî'kâ â'pui pui'dûng. Fowl four eggs laying are.	Four fowls are laying.
Pô'rôk â-nyî'kâ â'pui gûp dûng. Fowls two eggs sitting are.	Two fowls are sitting.
Tâg-ê-ing'kâ vông. Years ten past.	Ten years ago.
Ron'na ur'sing mur-ê-ing'kâ si'kâng. Rubber trees ten dead.	Ten rubber trees died.
Pâ-dâm'a sin'ying ê-lûng'em sô-ê'ing â-nyî'kâ pâ'tô. Abors this year boats twenty cut have.	The Abors cut twenty boats this year.
Ngâ shâ'ben â-nyî'lâ bâ-rê-ingk'â pâ'tô I goats two to rupees ten got.	I got two goats for ten rupees.
Lê'têr âb-dû'em pui'âk dôr-keng'kâ âp'tô. Once firing whilst crows six shoot have.	I shot six crows in one shot.

PRONOUNS.

7.—Personal Pronouns.

Ngâ gî-â'mâng. I come not.	I did not come.
Ngâ â-rô'pü tân'mâ. I truly hear not.	I do not believe it.
Nâ â-gin'pü ngâ'gdâ. You always late are.	You are always late.
Nâ lâ-bâg'na â-mî'a. You lazy man.	You are an idle fellow.
Nâ jîr-dû-na'yü ? You angry are ?	Are you angry ?
Nâ î-tô'yü ? You do have ?	Did you do it ?
Sim nâ kâng-ken-dâ'yü ? This you know ?	Do you know this ?

Bui bâr-pi'kâ em'dûng. He rupees four saying.	He asks rupees four.
Bui gî-lat-dâk-kû'vông. He turn back has.	He has turned back.
Nâ bâng ken-pui'â? You swim know to?	Can you swim?
Nâ kî-lâ-pui'â? You count able are?	Can you count?
Bû'lûm bî-lâng'kâ. Them to give.	Give it to them.
Ngâ bû'lûm lû'tô. I them to say have.	*I* told them.
Bû'lû mâk'shâ shâ'dûng. They dancing are.	*They* are dancing.
Bû-lû'ka âm'a min-kâ'vô. Their "dhan" ripened has.	*Their* "dhan" is ripe.
Ngâ-lû'ka âm'a min'mâ. Our "dhan" ripe not.	*Our* "dhan" is not ripe.
Bui'ka ê-k'ia lê-vê'dâk. His dog lame is.	*His* dog is lame.
Ngâ'lû Mî-shing'a â'sî â-nin'lâ yê'dâ. We Miris water near to live.	*We* Miris live near the water.
Nâ'lû kô kî-din'ga â-gin'pü shâ-mân-dûng. You children always playing are.	*You* children are always playing.

8.—Relative Pronouns.

Â-lü'lâ gû'lî âb'nâm êk'î da. Neck in bullet shot dog it.	The dog *which* was shot in the neck.
Âm gân'nâm da jü'kâng. "Dhan" cut it wet became.	The dhan *which* was cut got wet.
Â'bûk âb'nâm â'mi da. Gun fired man he.	The man *that* fired the gun.
U'mü ûg'nâm * êk'um da Fire burnt house it.	The house *that* was burnt.
Lâm-bü'lâ † dir-kôm'na ur'si da. Road on broken tree it.	The tree *which* broke on the road.
Nâk tâ-lê'lâ gû'sôr § mô'na â'mi da. Your upon complaint maker man he.	The man *who* brought a case against you.
Lâ'lik î'na Pâ'dâm da. Reprisal maker Abor he.	The Abor *who* made the reprisal.
Gân'na ‡ ê'lû da. Sticker boat it.	The boat *which* ran aground.

* "g" substituted for "k" for sake of euphony.
† "kâm" is a particle denoting a covering up (*vide* ante).
"dîrkôm" means that the broken tree fell on or covered the road.
‡ "n" substituted for "t."

Ngôm gâ'lî * bî'na â'mî da Me to abuse giver man he.	The man *that* abused me.
Â-lê'lâ ngôm nig'na or da Leg in me pricker "panji" it yông-mô-dûng'ai. poisoned was.	The "panji" *which* pierced my foot was poisoned.
Ben'na gâ'sôr da. Torn cloth it.	The cloth *which* was torn.

9.—Interrogative Pronouns.

A-gin'em sê'kô bôm-kâ'na? Axe who taken?	*Who* has taken (away) the axe?
Sî â'mî sî sê-kô'na.? This man this who?	*Who* is this man?
Nâ sêk'ôm bî-tô'na? You who to given have?	To *whom* did you give it?
Ngâ sê-ka'lok âm-buin'em lâ yê'na? I whose from rice take shall? (possession)	*From whom* shall I get the rice?
In kâ'lâ ai-yâ dâ'na? Which better is?	*Which* is the best?
Sâk mî'dûm † ân'yî sâk These from men two these from sê'kô nôm pâ-tô'na? who you strike has?	*Which* of these two men struck you?
Bui kâ-pî'na â-mî'a? He what kind of man?	*What kind of* a man is he?
Bui nôm kâ'pü pâ-tô'na? He you what manner strike has?	*How* did he strike you?
Nâ â'lô a-dit'kâ lâ'pü You salt, how much take to mui-dû'na? wishing are?	*How much* salt do you want?
Da lâ'ê-lûn'ga a-dit'kâ dû'na? There boats how many are?	*How many* boats are there there?
Nâ sâ a-dit'kâ gî-âng-kâ'na? You here how many came?	*How many* times have you been here?
Pô-lô'lâ nôm a-dit'kâ Month in you to how many mur-kông'em bî-yê'na? rupees give shall?	*How much* shall I pay you a month?
Nâ'ka â'min in-qua'na? Your name what?	*What* is your name?
A'la in'qua ngôm-dû'na? There what noise is?	*What* noise is that?
In'kâ lê-gâng'a gê-muin-shû-dû'na? What cause quarrelling are?	*What* is the cause of this quarrel?

* Assamese words.

† This word is often used in lieu of "âmi," when two or three men are being spoken of.

Sì lâm'bü sì in-kâ'lâ pui-dû'na ? This road this where reaches ?	*Where* does this road lead ?
Nâ in'kom mâ-tâ-dû'na ? You what searching are ?	*What* are you seeking ?
Ngâ da'pü a-dì'lô lû-kâ'na ? I that wise when said?	*When* did I say so ?
Yûm'râ pa-jâ'ba a-dì'ló Jungle (*i.e.*,) wild ducks when pui-dâ'na ? arrive ?	*When* do the wild ducks come in ?
Nâ a-dì'lô . kì-kâ'na ? You when ill have been ?	*When* were you ill ?

10.—Demonstrative Pronouns.

Sì tâ'bui sì kì'pâr kê-êg'lâ This snake this dhan pounder beneath dûng'ai. was.	*This* snake was underneath the "dhan" pounder.
Sim tâ'bui sim mô-kê'to-kâ. This snake this kill.	Kill *this* snake.
Sì dûm'lûp sì sâ'ka Pâ'dâm sâ-ko'dì This hat this this of Abor this of a'lok Mì'dì a-lok-a'dì ? that there } from Mishmi that there from ?	Does *this* hat belong to this Abor or that Mishmi ?
Da â'mì da Mì-dì'a. That man that Mishmi.	*That* man is a Mishmi.
Dem Mì'shing kì'dì dem â-pông'em Those Miris those liquors bì-lâng'ka. give.	Give *those* Miris liquor.
Dâk â'mì dâk bui That from man that from he lâ-lik-tô-na'yü? reprisal has ?	Did he make the reprisal *from that* man ?
Sì'da kô mil'vô sì'da This (very) boy this (very) ngâ'ka ê-kì'em tû'to. my dog kicked.	*This* (very) boy kicked my dog.
Sì'dem âm'buin sì'dem ngâ kâ'pü This rice this I how ma-lik-lâ-yê'na ? send able shall (be) ?	How shall I be able to send *this* rice ?
A da kô mil'vô da ê'lûng â-sì'em That boy that boat water kâr-buin-mô'to-kâ. throw out make.	Make *that* boy throw the water out of the boat.
A dem â'rê dem ngâ ma'lô That (very) horn that I yesterday lâng-gê'ma em'tô. take will not said.	*That* (very) horn I refused yesterday.

The indefinite pronouns do not require any further illustrating.

12.—VERBS.

Miri	Literal	English
Dâ'nyî kê-shâ'pü ûn'dâk.	Sun similarly shining is.	It shines like the sun.
Bôg-râ'lâ sî-mo'na dûng.	"Chupri" on deer are.	There are deer on the "Chupri."
Sim sî'râ âm'a bâ-jê'kâ dûng dâ-pô'num.	Nowadays "dhan" much is eat to.	Nowadays there is lots of rice to eat.
Pô-lô'a shâ'dak.	Moon rising is.	The moon is rising.
Ê-kum'em ü'mü ûk'dûng.	House fire burning is.	The house is on fire.
Nâ in'kôm nâm-kî*-dû'na?	You what smelling are?	What are you smelling?
Â-si'a ai-rû'pü ân-chî-dûng'ai.	Water very cold was.	The water was very cold.
Bôm-pô'nâm† kô'pâk da ai-dûng'ai.	First brought plantains they good were.	The first plantains brought were good.
Nâ pa-shâ-dâ'yü?	You afraid are?	Are you afraid?
Bui lê'kô‡ lê'kô pông‡-kok'lâ gî'dâ.	He at intervals comes.	He comes sometimes.
Ngâ pet-pâk'tô?	I torn have?	I have torn (it).
Tâng'a ngôm nik'tô.	Thorn me pricked has.	A thorn has pricked me.
Ngâ buim ai'pü î'tô.	I him cured have.	I have cured him.
Nâ mai-nâm'pü lû'tô.	You falsely spoken have.	You have spoken falsely.
Bui sim-yâ'kô âp'tô.	He tiger shot has.	He has shot a tiger.
Bû'lû sî'mon â-sik'em di'tô.	They deer skin taken off have.	They have skinned the deer.
Nâ â-pin'em mô-tô'yü?	You rice cooked have?	Have you cooked the rice?

* Compound word "nâm"=smell, "kî"=measure.

† "bômnâm"=past participle passive of root verb "bôm"=bring, with the particle of priority, "pô," added.

‡ "lêkô"=once, "pông-koklâ"=lit., midway.

Ur-sî-lok'ka oi-dâ-kû'dem* Tree from descending while bui ô-let'kâng. he fell.	He fell while descending from the tree.
A-gin'em sê'kô bôm-kâ'na? Axe who taken has?	Who has taken the axe?
Ur'sî teng-kâ'yü? Trees cut have?	Did you cut the trees?
Bû'lû rôn'nô pâ'yê. They rubber cut will.	They will cut rubber.
Bui nôm ê-lûng'em bi'yê. He you boat give will.	He will give you the boat.
Ngâ yam'pô ki-ki'pü. I morrow measure will.	I will measure it to-morrow.
Long'a ki-nit'kâ dûng-gê'lâ bû'lû Days seven waiting they â'reg ü'mü bâ'yê. fields fire light will.	They will burn (their) fields seven days hence.
Ngâ nôm yâm'pô bi'pü. I you morrow give will.	I will give it to you to-morrow.
Nâ a-dî'lô gî-lai-yê-kû'na? You when return will?	When will you return?
Nâ sî'lô î-pu'iâ yâm'pô You this day do will morrow î-pu'iâ? do will?	Will you do it to-day, or to-morrow?
Ân-jâ'kâ tê-mui'lô kê-mô-yê'pü. Little stay if dark will become.	It will be dark shortly.
Nâ'ka dâ-lû'lâ sî'lô pui-pui'â? Your village to this day reach will?	Shall you reach your village to-day.
Min-dâ-rî'a nôm gâ-pü'kü. Cat you scratch will.	The cat will scratch you.
U-mü'a nôm ûk-pü'kü. Fire you burn will.	The fire will burn you.
Ngâ â'bûk bê-nâm'em tât-veg'dâ. I gun noise hear can.	I can hear the report of the gun.
Ngâ â'sî kê-êg'bôk ur-ling'em I water below from stones kâ-lâ'pü. see able am.	I can see the stones at the bottom of the water.
Ngâ â-di'lâ shâ-lâ'pü. I mountain up mount able am.	I can climb a mountain.
Ngâ ur-sî'lâ rê-shâ-lâ'mâ? I tree up climb able not?	I cannot climb a tree.
Nâ ur-sî'lâ rê-shâ-lâ-pui'â? You tree up climb able are?	Can you climb a tree?
Nâ ai-ô'pü sim'yâ â-sik'em You well tiger skin dî-lâ-pui'â? take off able are?	Can you skin a tiger well?

* "oi-dâ-kûdem=lit., while descending *again*.

Miri / literal	Translation
Ngâ'ka â-lâk'a gât-shû-mâ-dâ'dem â'gêr î-lâ dûng'ai. My hand cut not while work do able was.	Before I cut my hand I was able to work.
Ngâ tü-ling-â' muilô sî-da'na â-pông'em tü-pui'ai. I thirsty was if this much liquor drink would.	If I was thirsty, I would drink this much liquor.
Ngâ'ka â-lê'a dir-mâng-â'mui"lô ngâ gî-gôr-lâ-pui'ai. My leg break not had if I walk able would be.	If I had not broken my leg, I would have been able to walk.
Ngâ yâm'pô gi-lâ yê'pü. I morrow go able will be.	I shall be able to go to-morrow.
Sî-môn'em kâ-veg-â'mui"lô bui âp-pui'ai. Deer seen had if he shoot would.	Had he seen the deer, he would have shot it.
Mai-nâ'pü gî-â-lâng'kâ. Quickly come.	Come quickly.
Ôg-yüm'lâ ma'to-kâ. Shade in put.	Put it in the shade.
U-mü'em mô-mit'to-kâ. Fire put out.	Put out the fire.
Nâ'ka dûm'wit dem shûm'to-kâ. Your hair it fasten up.	Tie up your hair.
Sim ât'târ sim kâ-tô-î'kâ. These things these look after.	Look after these things.
Sê-kôm-at'ê lûyô-kâ. Any one at all say not.	Do not tell any one.
Â-gôm'a lû'yô-kâ. Words speak not.	Do not speak.
Bû'lû â-mî'em yü-kâ'pü gî'kâng. They man bury purpose of gone.	They have gone (for) to bury the man.
Gû'lî âb'nâm sî'mon dem bui mâ-tâ-kâ'pü. Bullet shot deer it he search for gone.	He has gone to look for the wounded deer.
Bui bui'ka bui-râ'em gi-rik-kâ'pü gî-dâk. She her brother meet purpose of going is.	She is going to meet her brother
Âm gât-dâ'dem ngâ tâ-bui'em kâ'tô. Dhan cutting while I snake saw.	I saw a snake while cutting the paddy.
Â'sî kô-dâ'dem bui â-sî'lâ sî kâng. Water crossing whilst he water in died.	He was drowned while crossing the river.

Yôk′shik pui-dâ′dem ngâ′ka Knife sharpening whilst my â-lâk′em gât-shû′tô. finger cut have.	I cut my finger while sharpening the knife.
Sim′yâ kâ′lâ ngâ dûk′tô. Tiger seeing I run have.	Seeing the tiger I ran away.
Ngâ-lû′ka â′reg ri-gû-mô-âm′lâ Our fields weeding finish having sim sî′râ ân-jâ′kâ dû-pâ′dûng. at present little sit may.	Having finished weeding our fields, we may rest a little.
Nê′yâng ki′di da bû′lâ yôp-pâk′te-kâ. Weeds them plucking throw away.	Pull up the weeds and throw them away.
Mai-nâ′pü dûg′lâ lâ′tô-kâkâ. Quickly running fetch.	Run quickly and fetch it.

14. Causative Verbs.

Ur′sing yün′to-kâ. Tree shake.	Shake the tree.
Ngôm â′bûk âv-yîr-yî′kâ. Me gun shoot teach.	Teach me how to fire a gun.
Sim âmb′uin sim pôm′to-kâ This rice this soak.	Soak this rice.
Nôm â-mî′em pâ-mô′pü You person beat make will.	I will have you beaten.

15.—Compound Verbs.

Nâ ê-lûng′em yâm-kî-tô′yü? You boat fathomed have?	Have you fathomed the boat?
Men-jâ′ka buim â-rê′lok ât-pâk′tô. Buffalo him horns with tossed has.	The buffalo tossed him.
Nâ′lû Pâ-dâma kâ-pi′lâ â-ginpü You Abors why always lâ′lik î-dû′na? reprisals doing are?	Why are you Abors always making reprisals.
Sû′pâk ngâ gâ-lûk′em gê-ki-lâ′mâ. Now I jacket try on able not.	I cannot try on the jacket now.
Lâm-bü′em gî-mûr-shû′yô-kâ.* Road mistake not.	Do not lose your way.
Ngâ′ka â-pông′em tüng-ki′to-kâ. My liquor taste.	Taste my liquor.

18.—ADVERBS.

Nâ dâ′muir muir-nâm′em You thundering tât-veg-mâ-lân′gâ? hear can not?	Do you not hear the thunder?

* "gi"=go, "mûr"=mistake; "gîmûr" would be equivalent to the English word *lose*, as here used.

A'lem tâ'bui a'lem nâ **That (there) snake that you** **kâ-veg-mâ-lân'gâ?** **see can not?**	**Do you not see that snake?**
Nâ buim kâng-ken-mâ-lân'gâ? **You him know not?**	**Do you not recognise him?**
Nâ mâk'shâ shâ'pü mui-mâ-lân'gâ? **You dance to wish not?**	**Do you not wish to dance?**
Nâ gî'pu mui-mâ-lân'gâ? **You go to wish not?**	**Do you not wish to go?**
Rî'gû mô-in-mâ'lâ ngâ gî-lâ'mâ. **Weeding finished not I go able not.**	**Not having finished our weeding, I cannot go.**
Â'bûk bôm-mâ'lâ si-mon'em **Gun carry not having deer** **âb-lâ-tô'mâng.** **shoot able have not been.**	**Not having carried a gun, I could not shoot the deer.**
Pô'dông ô-yê-mui'lo ngâ **Rain fall will if I** **gî-âng-gê'mâ.** **come will not.**	**If it rains, I will not come.**
Bui gî-â-mâ'mui"lô ngâ gôk-kâ'pü **He come not if I call purpose of** **gî'pu.** **go will.**	**If he does not come, I will go (for) to call him.**
Ngâ î-âm-mâng'âdâ. **I do completed not yet.**	**I have not yet finished.**
Bui lông-kâ'tê dû'mâ. **He day one even stay not.**	**He did not stay even one day.**

19.—ADVERBS.

Nâ in-kâ'lâ gî-yê'na? **You where go will?**	**Where are you going to?**
Yâ'lâ ngâ kâ'pü kâ-yê'na? **Night in I how see shall?**	**How shall I see in the night.**
Mô'yăm bâ-jê-rûng'kâ pô'dông **Last evening much very rain** **ô'ka.** **fell.**	**Last evening *very much* rain fell.**
Sû'pâk gî-dân*-kâ-lâng'kâ. **Now go at once.**	**Go *at once.***
Pâ-dâm'a lê-kô'pü gî-âng'kâ. **Abors together came.**	**The Abors came altogether.**
Â-mî'kâ â-tê'rê gî-lât-kâng'kû. **Man one alone returned.**	**One man returned *alone.***
Ngâ'lû si'mon â-têr-â'kâ kâ'tô. **We deer one only saw.**	**We saw one deer *only.***
A-m'ia â-têr-â'kâ gî-âng'kâ. **Man one only come has.**	**One man *only* has come.**

* "dân" a particle denoting celerity.

Nâ'ka â'bûk lê-têr-â'kâ âp-kî'to-kâ. Your gun once only fire.	Fire your gun once *only*.
Ngôm si-di'kâ bî-pui'â da-dî'kâ bî-pu'iâ? Me to this much give will that much give will?	Will you give me *this much* or *that much*?
Deng-um'pü gî'to-kâ ngâ'ka â'lê kî'dûng. Slowly go my foot sore is.	Go *slowly*, my foot is sore.
Ngâ â-rô'pü yâm'pô gî-â'pu. I truly morrow come will.	I will really come to-morrow.
Yâ'rî gâr-dâ'dem ur'sing kê-êg'lâ dû'yô-kâ. Lightning flashing (?) whilst tree beneath sit not.	Do not sit under a tree when it is lightning.
Ngâ'ka kê-râ'pü gî'to-kâ. My front go.	Walk on before me.
Kê'mô mâng-â-dâ'pü ê-kûm'lâ gî-kâ-lâng-kû'kâ. Dark not still house to go.	Go home before it is dark.
Â'pui dâ-mâng-â-dâ'pü ngâ gî'kâ. Rice eat not yet I went.	I went before I had eaten.
Bui'ka ê-kum'a dâ-lûng râ-dâ'lâ dûng. His house village centre in is.	His house is in the middle of the village.
Sin'ying ngâ-lû'ka âm'a ai'mâ sin mâ ai'dâk sin mâ. This year our dhan good not also not good is also not.	Our dhan is neither good nor bad this year.
Ngâ'ka ma-ang'a kî'dûng dê-pi'lâ ngâ gî-lâ'mâ. My wife will is therefore I go able not.	My wife is ill, therefore I cannot go.
Tâ-pâm'a ô'kâng, dê-pi'lâ ân-chin'ga. Snow fallen, therefore cold.	Snow has fallen, therefore it is cold.
Nâ ai'pü ni'tôm mô* ken-dâ'yü? You well sing make know?	Can you sing well?

* "nitôm mô"=sing, lit., make sing.

MISCELLANEOUS PHRASES.

Travel.

Miri (with interlinear gloss)	English
Ngâ â-nin'na Pâ'dâm dâ-lû'lâ I near Abor villages kâng-kâ'pü gî'pü yâmpô see purpose of go will morrow Sâ-dî â sâk'ka rô-kôm'pü ê-lû'lâ Sadiya from early morning boat in gî'pü. go will.	I am going to visit some of the near Abor villages. I shall leave Sadiya by boat very early to-morrow.
Nâ-ka'lâ si'pâi gî-vô-pui'â, You with sepoys accompany will, e'lû mô'pü Mî-shing'em boat work to Miris gî-vô-yê-na'yü Dû-mi'em gî-vô-yê- go will Dumes go with nâ'yü? will?	Will you take any sepoys with you, (and) will you take Miris or Dumes to work the boat?
Ngâ sî'pâi ân'yi â-ûm'kâ gî-vô'pü I sepoys two three go with will ê'lû mô'na Mîshing gî-vô'pü. boat workers Miris go with will.	I shall only take two or three sepoys, (and) I shall have Miris to work the boat.
Mai-nâ'pü ât'târ â-puing'em ê-lû'lâ Quickly things all boat in reb-lik-âm'to-kâ ngâ'ka â-bûk'em fill completely my guns ai-ô'pü kâ-lâng'ka. carefully took to.	Be quick. Put everything in the boat, and take special care of my guns.
Ngâ-lû'ka ê-lûng'a mai-nâ'pü Our boat quickly tok-pô'dâ. downstream goes.	We are going downstream very fast.
A! sî'râ â-si'a ai-rû'pü Yes! this morning water very bid'dâk â-dî'lâ bâ'jê pô'dông swift hills in much rain ô'kâ tâ-pâm'a tê jit'dûng fallen, snows also melting are.	Yes! the current is very strong this morning. Much rain has fallen in the hills, and the snows are melting.
Â'sî bôg'gâ dem tû-shâ'lâ ngâ'lû River mouth it turning we shâ-yê-na'yü? upstream (go) shall?	After passing the mouth of the river, shall we go upstream?
A! shâ'yê â-sî'lâ Yes! up stream shall water in shü-tûng-â'pü. snags only.	Yes! (and) the water is all snags.
Sî'lo ngâ'lû Mê'bô pui-gâ'lâ This day we Membo "ghat" to pui-yê'di? arrive shall?	Shall we reach the Membo ghat to-day?

A! dâ ′nyî lô-ing-mui ′lô pui-yê′dî Yes! sun full when arrive shall?	Yes! at midday.
Kô-tô′ki â-nyî′kâ dâ-lû′lâ ma-lik ′to- Kotokis two village to send kâ bâ-ta ′na gâm ki-ding′em lû ′to-kâ big "gams" inform Sâ-he ′ba gî ′dâ em′to-kâ. Saheb comes say.	Send two kotokis to Membo, and inform the head "gams" of my arrival.
Ngâ ′lû dâ-lû ′lâ gî ′lâ gâm′êm We village to going gams lû-bî ′tô Sâ-heb ′a gî ′da em ′tô told have Saheb comes said have.	We have been to the village, and informed the gams of your arrival.
Bû ′lû ai-rû ′pü â-sa-dûng ′ai bû ′lû They very pleased were, they Pâ-dâm ′em ê ′ing â-nyî ′kâ Sâ ′heb Abors twenty saheb ât-târ ′em jâ-yê ′pü em ′nâ ma-lik′tô. things carry will saying sent have	They were very pleased (and) have sent twenty Abors to carry your things.
Lâm ′bü yüm ′râ dû ′dî pa ′jî dû ′dî? Road jungle is sting nettles is?	Is there any jungle or sting-nettles on the road?
Ma! Lâm-bü ′em pâ ′tûng pa′jî No! road cut has been sting nettle sin kâ mâng tâ ′pât sin kâ ′mâng. even exists not leeches even exist not.	No! The road has been cleared and there are neither sting nettles or leeches.
Nâ-lû ′ka dâ lûng lü-pû ′na Your village goitre people â-râng ′a. full of.	You have a deal of goitre in your village.
A! nâ lü pü kû-shê ′rî bôm-tû Yes! you goitre medicine brought yü? lü-pû ′na tâ-kâm ′a have? goitre people every one nâ-ka ′lâ kû-shê ′rî kô-kâ ′pü you to medicine asking for gî-â-yê′pü. come will.	Yes? Have you brought any goitre ointment? All the people with goitre will be asking for it (soon).
Nâ-lûk ′a bô′rê mûr-kông ′em Your "posa" rupees or-shû-tô-vô′yü? distribute have?	Have you distributed your village "posa"?
A! or-shû-tô ′vông Yes! distributed has been pui ′mâ Lüng ′â (but is) insufficient, five hundred mûr ′kô da sî-dan ′a â ′mî rupees they this many people sim pui-yê-lân ′gâ? this suffice will?	Yes! (but) it is insufficient. Will Rs. 500 suffice for this number people?

<table>
<tr><td>Nâ-lû'ka â'rêg ê-tôr'a ai-rû'pü
Your field fences very
ai'dâk
good are.</td><td>What good fences you make to your fields.</td></tr>
<tr><td>Ngâ'lû ai-rû'pü mô-mâ-mui'lô
We well make not if
ur-sâ'a sin si-mon'a sin âm'em
"mithon" also deer also dhan
dâ-pü'kü.
eat will.</td><td>If we did not make them good, the "mithon" and deer would eat our "dhan."</td></tr>
<tr><td>Nâ'lû Pâ'dâm si kâ-pi'lâ â-gin'pü
You Abors why always
lâ'lik i-kû-i-yü-dâ'na?
reprisals making.</td><td>Why are you Abors always making reprisals.</td></tr>
<tr><td>Ngâ-lû'ka i-kâm'a.
Our practice.</td><td>It is our custom.</td></tr>
<tr><td>Nâ-lû'ka pâk'bô pâng'na
Your slaves male slaves female
bâ-jê kâ dû-na'yü?
many are?</td><td>Have you many slaves?</td></tr>
<tr><td>A! mûr'kông kân'na dûng.
Yes! (lit.) rupee possessors are.</td><td>Yes! The wealthy have them.</td></tr>
<tr><td>Bû'lû ai'ka rû-tûm'lâ lê-kô'pü
They their masters with together.
dû-dâ'yü?
stay?</td><td>Do they live together with their masters?</td></tr>
<tr><td>Nâ-lû'ka mur-muin'em in-kâ'lok
Your touchwood where from
pâ-dâ'na?
get?</td><td>Where do you get your touchwood from?</td></tr>
<tr><td>Tâ'mâk ur-si'lok pâ'dâ.
Shewa tree from get.</td><td>We get it from the Shewa tree.</td></tr>
<tr><td>Mê'bô Pâ-dâm'a ên'gâ mô-dâ'yü?
Membo Abors fish catch?
tem'pü log'yü ê'lû log'yü mô-dâ'na?
land from boat from catch?</td><td>Do the Membo Abors catch fish, (and if so) do they catch them in boats or from the bank?</td></tr>
<tr><td>A! ngâ'lû ê-ngâ'em tem-pü'lok
Yes! we fish land from
mô'dâ. Ngâ'lû ê'lû mô-ken'mâ.
catch. We boat work understand not.</td><td>Yes! We catch fish from the bank. We do not know how to work a boat.</td></tr>
<tr><td>Si'âng â-si'lâ â'kô â'kô bû'teng ai'mâ.
Dihong water in some rapids good not.</td><td>The Dihong has some nasty rapids.</td></tr>
<tr><td>A'ieng Pâ'dû pui'gâ sôk'kâ
Aiyeng Padoo ghat below
(lit., downstream).
da bû'teng ai-rû'pü ai-mâ-na'kâ
it rapid very bad one
(lit., not good).
dûng dâ'ka bû'tê dâ'ka â-min'a Pâk'puit.
is its rapid its name Pakpuit.</td><td>Just below the Aiyeng Padoo "ghat" there is a very bad one, called the Pakpuit.</td></tr>
</table>

Sì ur'jâ sì sê-kô'na ? This old woman this who ?	Who is this old woman ?
Ngâ'ka â-nyî'a da ngâ'ka My mother-in-law that my ô'ma mâk-bô'a. son-in-law.	My mother-in-law. That is my son-in-law.
A'la sî'kû ê'gâ a'lem lông That (there) Siku bridge that days a-dit'kâ mô-tô'na ? how many made has ?	How long did it take to make that bridge over the Siku.
Lô ê'ing â-nyî'kâ mô'tô ling'kâ Days twenty made has one hundred â-mî'a dem mô-dûng'ai. men it making were.	Twenty days (and) there were one hundred men working.
Dû'tâk dû-tâk'lâ nâ'lû mô-ten-dâ'yü ? Yearly you repair (it) ?	Do you repair it yearly?
Nâ-lû'ka â-re'ga dâ-lû'lok mô-tê'dâk. Your fields village from far are.	Your fields are a long way from your village.
A ! ngâ'lû â'mî bâ-je'lâ â'reg î'kô* Yes ! we people many being cultivating kâ-muin-shû-mâ'lâ† space existing in proximity not mô-tê'pü â'kô â'kô î'dâ. far off some cultivate (lit., do).	Yes ! We are so many souls that some must go far off. (to cultivate).
Mô tê'pü â'reg î'na‡ kî'dî da âm Far off cultivators they "dhan" gât-dû'em ri'gû mô-dû'em â-reg'lâ cutting whilst weeding whilst fields in yŭp-dâ'yŭ ? sleep do?	Do the people who have their fields so far away sleep out in the busy season.
Nâ-lû'ka dâ-lû'lâ gî-dâ'dem Your village to coming whilst kî'rûp rûng'na â'mî gî-rik-shû'tô. hunting party met have. Ngâ'ka gî-rik-shû-dâd'em bû'lû â-tî-kô' My meeting while they anything sin pâtô-mâ. at all got have not.	While coming to your village I met a hunting party. When I met them, they had got nothing.
Bû-lû'ka gî'jon da'lok â'mî Their companions them from man â'kâ sî'tûm bâ-tê-rûna'kâ lâng one bear large very one and yi-rôm'kâ kâ-tû'ai em'nâ ngôm lû'tô. pig tusker saw saying me to said.	One of their party told me he had seen a large bear and a tusker pig.

---

* "â reg î"=cultivate.

† "kâ="exists not, muinshû"=reflexive, reciprocative particle with negative particle "mâ," and participial "lâ."

‡ "âreg î na"=lit., field doors (the "na" is the adjectival "na.)

Nâ-lû'ka Pâ'dâm sí'na â-mi'em kâ'pü Your Abor dead people how yŭ-dâ'na? bury do?	How do you Abors bury your dead?
Ngâ'lû sí'na â-mi'em tet-tû-mô-tû'lâ We dead people sitting position yŭ dâ. (in) putting bury do.	We bury them in a sitting position.
Nâ-lû'ka yông-mô'em in-kâ'lok Your poison where from pâ-dâ'na? get do?	Where do you get your poison from?
Ê-pûk'lâ yông'mô tî-lik-yê'mui'lô Arrow on poison apply will if a-dit'kâ ai'pü dâg-yê'na? how long good remain will?	How long will it last good when applied to an arrow.
Kî'rûp dâ'dem nâ'lû ê-kí'em gî-vô-dâ'yü Hunting whilst you dogs accompany permit do.	Do you take dogs with you while hunting.
Bê'lâng â-pui'kâ* puir'to-kâ. Jack one pick.	Pick me a jack.
Nâ'lû a-dî'lô kê'bâ† bâ-dâ'na? You when council hold?	When do you hold council.
A'jeng kâ'em‡ bâ'dâ dâ-pî-ô'em Cases occurring if assemble theft occur- kê'bâ bâ'dâ â'reg ring if assemble; lit., field âm âm-sâm-î'em ô'yû "dhan" withering if spirits î-lâ'jê § em'nâ kê'bâ consult lets saying council bâ'dâ. assemble.	When there is any case. If a theft occurs we sit; if our dhan withers we sit in order to consult and propitiate the spirits.
Nâ-lû'ka Pâ-dâm'a â'kô â'kô tûb- Your Abors some bald lôk-dâ'yü? are?	Do some Abors get bald?
Ngâ-lû'ka â'mô sâk nâ'lû in'quâ in'quâ Our territory from you what what ât-târ'em rê-dâ'na? articles purchase do?	What goods do you purchase from us?

---

* "âpui"=numeral affix, with "kâ" affixed.
† "kêbâ bâto-kâ"=assemble council.
‡ "âjeng kâem"=lit., if a case happens.
§ "ôyü î-lâjê"=lit., let us *do* spirits.

Ngâ'lû â-lô'em sin rê'dâ We salt also purchase yôk-din'em sin rê'dâ iron also purchase tâ-dôk'em tê rê'dâ kû-yâp'em beads also purchase, now tê rê'dâ tâ'pûm gû-sôr'- also purchase silkworm cloth em tê rê'dâ tô'em tê also purchase "tows" also rê'dâ â'tî tâ-kâm'em purchase articles all rê'dâ. purchase.	We purchase salt, also iron, also beads, also silkworm cloth, also "tows" (in fact) we buy everything.
Nâ-lû'ka â-dî'lâ tâ-pâm'em ô-dâ'yü? Your hill in snow falls?	Does it snow in your hills?
Sim ur'sî sim nâ'lû kâ-pi'lâ These trees these you why pâ-rek-tô'na? rung have?	Why have you rung these trees?
Lâm-bu'a ai-rû'pü per-mûk'dak Road very dust is.	The road is very dusty.
Bâ'jê nâng'âr ô'dûng. Much dew falling is.	Much dew is falling.
Mân mî'mâk pâ-muin-shû'nâm Burmah battle fought nâ ken-dâ'yü? you know?	Do you remember the Burmese war?
A'da ê'kum dem a-dî'lô ât-tô'na? That house that when pull down have?	When did you pull down that house?
Ngâ'ka gî-yê'kû lông'em nâ-lû'ka My returning day your kô kî-ding'em â-mân'em bî- children present give pü. will.	On the day of my departure I will give the children a small present.
Ngâ'ka gî-dâ-long-a'dem nôm My going day it you gôk'pü. call will.	On the day I start I will call you.
Sî'lô ngâ'ka gî-dâ-kû'dem This day my going back whilst sî'na sî-mon'em lâm-bü'lâ dead deer road on kâ'tô. seen have.	To-day while going (along), I saw a dead deer on the road.
Si'da â'mi sî'da ngâ-lû'ka yông'mô. This man this our blacksmith.	This man is our blacksmith.

Bui mât-shik'em sin yôk-tûm'em* sin He "daos" also yoke tooms, also ken-tû'em sin pâg-râng'em† earrings, also leaden earrings, sin yôk-shik'em sin shâ-mâk'em also knives also flintstrikers sin ân'gü ân'gü ât-târ'em sin also other things also mô'dâ. makes.	He makes "daos," also "yoke-tooms," also earrings, also "pag-rangs,"† also knives, also flint strikers (and) other things.
Sî'da bui'ka mât-dûn'ga. These his bellows.	These are his bellows.
Nâ'lû Pâ-dâm'a kâ'pü pê-shû dâ'na? You Abors how oath administer?	How do you Abors administer an oath ?
Â-kon'em da'pü dân'yi pô'lô ngôm One (way) that wise sun moon me dâ-yê'pü ngâ mai-nâm'pü lûmem- eat will I falsely speaking dû'mui"lô. am if.	One way is this, the sun (and) moon will eat me if I am speaking falsely.
Pâ-dâm'a bâ-jê'kâ bân ken-dâ'yü? Abors many swin know?	Can many Abors swim ?
Mâ! a'nyî â-ûm-â'kâ bân ken-dâ. No! two three only swim know.	No ! only two or three.
Bû'lû â-sî'em tê dûr ken-dâ'yü? They water also dive know?	Can they dive also?
Ngâ â'sî dûr ken'dâ. Sû'pâk ngâ I water dive know. Now I dûr'lâ a'la ur'ling a'lem lâ-sâ-la' diving that stone that lift able pü. will.	I can dive. I will do so now, and will be able to pick up that stone.
Ngâ'ka lû'nâm ur'lî dem My spoken stone it kâ-veg-dâ'yü? see can?	Do you see the one I mean ?

* "Yôktûm" is a sort of "dao" made by the Abors.

† Note.—"Pâgrâng" is a kind of earring worn (in the lobe of the ear) by Abor women from Damroh Padam, and villages to the north of it. (Abor women from villages nearer than Damroh Padam do not wear them.) It is made (of stuff resembling lead) in one continuous coil, something after the fashion of a snake bracelet, and they are often of great weight. I once weighed one, and found it over ½lb avoirdupois.) Women wearing them walk with a distinctly visible bend of the head forward, which looks strained and unnatural. I am told that the stuff is valuable, and that none but the relations of wealthy people can afford them.

A'la mi'ma a'lem pü nâ-lû'ka That woman that like your mi'ma â-puing'a tâ'li* women all "tali" ga-dâ'yü? wear?	Do all your woman carry like that one, *viz.*, on the head.
Nâ-lû'ka ê'kum â-kâp'em in-kâ'lok Your houses roofs what with kâp-dâ'na? roofed?	What are your houses roofed with?
Di-gin'lâ ê'sâr bâ-tê'em Cold weather in wind strong when nâ-lû'ka ê-kum'a ân-chi-mâ-lân'gâ? your houses cold not?	Are not your houses cold in the cold weather when it is windy?
Mi-ki'a nâ-lû'ka â-mîk'lâ dig-mâ- Smoke your eyes in smart lân'gâ? not? Â'mîk ki'na â-mi'em bâ-jê'kâ kâ'dâ. eyes sore people many see.	Does not the smoke hurt your eyes? I see many people with bad eyes.
A! da'pî dâk'kôm Yes! that so (*i.e.*, even so) being kâ-pi'yen? what shall we do?	Yes! what can we do?
Ma'yâ ngâ'ka ê-lûng'em â-si'a Last night my boat water yŭ-bôm'kâng. carried away.	Last night my boat was carried away by the current.
Nâ pâ-tô-kû-mâ-lân'gâ? You recover have not?	Did you not recover it?
A! pâ-tô'kû Dû-mi'a ê-lûng'em â'si Yes! recovered Dumes boat water yŭ-bîm-nâm'em ken'lâ ân-jâ'na carried away knowing small ê-lû'lok men-muin-gê'lâ boat with follow after having mô-tê'lok pâ-tô'kû. far from recovered.	Yes! I recovered it. The Dumes hearing of its having been carried off, went after it in a small boat, and recovered it a long way off.

Complaint.

Dû-mai'ka tâ-la'lâ gû'sôr Dumai against complaint mô-kâ'pü ô'yŭ-ka'lâ† ngâ make purpose of honour to I gi-â'dûng. come am.	I am come to your honour to complain against Dumai.

---

* "tali" is the name of the piece of bark used for carrying a basket.

† "ôyŭ" means a spirit. It is here used in much the same way as the Assamese use "dê-ôtâ."

Nâ inka gû-sô'rem lû-kâ'pü You what complaint speak purpose of **gî-dû'na?** come are?	**What complaint are you come to make?**
Bui ngâ'ka buir-ma'em rôl'lâ lâ'tô. He my sister seizing taken has.	**He has forcibly seized and carried off my sister.**
Bui in'kâ lê-gâ'lok da'pü He what account of that wise **î-tô'na?** done has?	**What is the reason of his having so acted?**
Ngâ bui'ka buir-ma'em lâ'tô* I his sister married **lâ-dâ'dem ngâ-lû'ka î-kâm'pü** marrying time of our custom to **ngâ'ka buir-ma'em â-lik'pü** my sister in exchange **bî'pü em-dûn'gai dêlo ânjâ-** give will agreed was then small **gâ'lok â-lik'pü bî'mâ** because in exchange give not **mê-lâm'pü.** afterwards.	**I married his sister, and at that time it was agreed that in accordance with our custom he was to have mine in exchange; but she was then young, and hence she was not then given in exchange (and) afterwards.**
Dû-mai'ka ân'gü ma-ang'a dûng Dumai other wife is **em'nâ buir-ma'em, bî-gê'mâ â'nü** saying sister, give will not mother **â-bû'a em'tô.** father said.	**Having ascertained that Dumai possessed another wife, my mother and father refused to give him my sister.**
Bíu'ka rôl'lâ gî-vô-kû-nâm'em. Her seizing taking off **â-mî'a kâ-tô'yü?** person see have?	**Did any one see him seize and carry off (the girl)?**
A! ân-jâ'kâ kê-mô-gâm-dâ'dem Yes! little dark somewhat whilst **bui ngâ-lû'ka ê'kum â-ninlâ.** he our house near to **gî-â'lâ ngâ'ka buin-ma'ka â-min'em** coming my sister's name **min'tô da'lo ngâ'ka yai'ô bui** called then my grandmother she **buim kâ'tô.** him seen has.	**Yes! my grandmother saw him do so. A little before dark coming close up to our house, he called my sister by name.**
Nâ'ka buir-ma'em âm'in min- Your sister name calling **dâ'dem. bui kâ'pü îtô'na?** whilst she what did? you **naken-dâ'yü?** know?	**What did your sister do when she heard her name called?**

---

* "yâmnê lâtô"=to take in marriage.

<table>
<tr><td>Ngá'ka buir'ma gôk-dû'di em'nâ
My brother call is saying
ngá'ka buir'ma in-gem'lâ
my sister outside
gi-len'kâng tât'dâ.
went (I) hear.</td><td>She went outside, thinking her brother had called her.</td></tr>
<tr><td>Da'lô Dû'mai bui nâ'ka buir-ma'em
Then Dumai he your sister
gâk-tô'yü?
seize has?</td><td>Was it then that Dumoi seized her?</td></tr>
<tr><td>A! Dû-mai'ka bui'ra â-nyî'kâ
Yes! Dûmai brothers two
tê bui-ka'lâ dûng'ai bû'lû sin
also his with was they also
buir-ma'em rôd-dûm-shû'tô.
sister seize helped.</td><td>Yes! Dumai's two brothers were also with him, (and) they also helped to seize my sister.</td></tr>
<tr><td>Bû'lû bu'im kâ'pü lâ-bôm-kâ'na?
They her from carry off did?</td><td>How did they take her away?</td></tr>
<tr><td>E-lû'lok Bû-lû'ka î-lûng'a dâ'lûng
Boat by their boat village
â'niu pui-gâ'lâ dûng'ai
near ghat at was</td><td>By boat. They had it at the "ghat," close to the village.</td></tr>
<tr><td>Nâ gâm ki-ding'em lû-tôy'ü?
You "gam'l told?</td><td>Have you spoken to the gams (about the matter)?</td></tr>
<tr><td>A! dâ lûng â-puing'a sim â'gôm
Yes? village all this affair
sim tat'pü em'nâ ma'lô
this enquire will saying yesterday
kê'bâ bâ-dûng'ai.
council assembled was</td><td>Yes! yesterday the whole village talked the matter over in council.</td></tr>
<tr><td>Bû'lû nôm kâ'pü î'to-ka em-tô'na?
They you what do tell have?</td><td>What did they advise you to do.</td></tr>
<tr><td>Ô-yü-ka'lâ gû'sôr mô-lang'kâ em'tô.
(Your) honour to complaint make
say have.</td><td>They advised me to complain to to your honour.</td></tr>
<tr><td>Dû'mai bui nâ'ka buir-ma'em
Dumai he your sister
in-kâ'lâ bôm'lâ lû-kâ'na?
where carrying hidden has?</td><td>Where has Dumai hidden your sister?</td></tr>
<tr><td>Nâp-shur'ka ê-kûm'lâ buir-ma'em
Napshur house in sister
lur-shû'tô tât'tô.
hidden has (I) heard.</td><td>He has, I bear, hidden her in Napshur village.</td></tr>
<tr><td>Châ! sû'pâk bû'lûm sâ'pü gâg'lâ
Very well now them here catching
gi-vô-lâng'kâ em'nâ ngâ lû-lik'pü.
bring with saying I send will.</td><td>All right (very well)! I will send and have them brought here.</td></tr>
<tr><td>Nâ'ka gû'sôr â-gôm'em âu-mô-tô'yü?
Your complaint written had have?</td><td>Have you had your complaint written out?</td></tr>
</table>

Mâ! ân-mâng-â'dâ sû'pâk No! written not yet now ân-mô'pü. written have will.	No! not yet; I will now do so.
Mai-nâ'pü ân-mô-lang'kâ nôm Quickly written have (it) you pê-shû-mô-gê'lâ nâ'ka â-gôm'em oath administering your words tât'pü. ask will.	Be quick (and) have it written; having made you take (an) oath; I will examine you.

VOCABULARY.

VOCABULARY.

English.	Shai′yâng Miri.	Abor.	Remarks.
Accompany, *v.*	Gî-muin.	Gî-muin.	"Gî"=go, "muin"=particle denoting with.
Adze (wood), *a.*	Lâp.	....	
Afterwards, *adv.*	Shû′gâm.	Shû′gâm.	*N.B.*—The roots only of the verbs appear in this vocabulary.
Again, *adv.*	Ê′gî *or* ê′gü.	Ê′gî *or* ê′gü.	
Against, *prep.*	Made by locative case post position "lâ."		
Air, *n.*	Ê′sâr.	Ê′sâr.	
Alligator, *n.*	Shâr′mon.	Shâr′mon.	
Alike, *a.*	Â-kâm′a.	Â-kâm′a.	
Alive, *a.*	Tûr′na.	Tûr′na.	
All, *a.*	Tâ-kâm′a.	Tâ-kâm′a.	
All right, very well	Châ.	Châ.	
Alone, *a.*	Â-têr′a.	Â-têr′a.	
Also, *adv.*	Sin *or* tê.	Sin *or* tê.	
Always, *adv.*	Â-gin′pü.	Â-gin′pü.	
Among, *prep.*	Râ′dâng.	Râ′dâng.	
And, *conj.*	Lâng.	Lâng.	
Anger, *v. t.*	Jîr.	Jîr.	
Anus, *n.*	Î′nâng *or* tâ′pông.	Î′nâng *or* tâ′pông.	
Ant, *n.*	Mê′râng.	Mê′râng *or* tâ′rûk.	
Aunt, *n.*	Nyâ′nî.	Nyâ′nî.	
Arm, *n.*	Â′lâk.	Â′lâk.	
Armpit, *n.*	Kî′rûng.	Kî′rûng.	

Arrived (at destination) *v.*	Pui-dâ'vô.	Pui-dâ'vô.	"Pui"=arrive, "dâ"=abbreviated form of substantive verb, and "vô"=completive particle.
Arrow, *n.*	Ê'pûk,	Ê'pûk.	
Ask, *v.*	Tan.	Tan.	
Ashes, *n.*	Mad'bû.	Mad'bû.	
Astonishing, to hear, *a.*	Tân-yi'ra.	Tân-yîr'a.	"Tâ"=root of verb to hear, "yîr"=root of verb to laugh.
Astonishing, to see *a.*	Kâng-yîr'a.	Kâng-yîr'a.	"Kâ"=root of verb to *see.*
Astringent, *a.*	Kê-nâm'a.	Kê-nâm'a.	
At, *prep.*	Made by a postposition "lâ."		
Axe, *n.*	Ê'ging.	Ê'ging.	
Awake, *v. t.*	Ût.	Ût.	
Awake, *v. i.*	Dâr.	Dâr.	
Bad, *a.*	Ai'mâ.	Ai'mâ.	lit., "ai"=good, "mâ"=not.
Bachelor, *n.*	Bâ-rô'lâng.	Bâ-rô'lâng.	Really Assamese word.
Back, *n.*	Lâm'kû.	Lâm'kû.	
Bag, *n.*	Yô'gon.	Yô'gon.	
Bald, *a.*	Tûb-lôk'a.	Tûb-lôk'a.	
Bank of river, *n.*	Râ'gô.	Râ'gô.	
Bamboo, *n.*	Dî'bâng.	Dî'bâng.	*Names of different kinds of bamboos.* Assamese. — Miri. jâti .... bâ'rô. kâkô .... ê'ôm. tâpû* .... ê'pô. bhûlû-kâ .... bû-lû'kâ. * Very large kind.
Bamboo *chunga,* *n.*	Dî'bâng ê'tûng.	Dî'bâng ê'tûng.	
Bark, *n.*	Ê'kî râ'nâm.	Ê'kî râ"nâm.	
Basket, *n.*	Ê'gin.	Ê'gin.	

English.	Shai-yâng Miri.	Abor.	Remarks.
Bat, *n.*	Tâk'pôn.	Tâk'pôn.	
Beard, *n.*	Nâm'mûr.	Nâm'mûr.	
Bear, *n.*	Sî'tûm.	Sî'tûm.	
Beat, *v.*	Pâ.	Pâ.	
Because, *conj.*	Made by using participial suffix "lâ" (*vide* Grammar).		
Beckon, *v.*	Ôg-yâp.	Ôg-yâp.	
Bee, *n.*	Tân'gût.	Tân'gût.	
Before (in front of), *adv.*	Kê-râ'pü.	Kê-râ'pü.	*In time previous*, is "kôjô."
Behind, last, *adv.*	Mê-lâm'pü.	Mê-lâm'pü.	
Belch, *v.*	Rê-vât.	Rê-vât.	
Belly, *n.*	Â'kî.	Â'kî.	
Bend, *v.*	Tûm-pîr.	Tûm-pîr.	
Be quiet.	Â'sô *or* Tai-em'a.	Âsô *or* Tai-em'a.	
Bheel, *n.*	Pâ'tâng.	Pâ'tâng.	
Bind (a man), *v.*	Yê.	Yê.	
Bind, or fasten animal, boat, &c., *v.*	Rin.	Rin.	
Bird, *n.*	Pret'tâng.	Pret'tâng.	
Birth, *n.*	Âu ô'nâm.	Âu ô'nâm.	
Bite, *v.*	Rek *or* Gâm.	Rek *or* Gâm.	
Bitter, *a.*	Kô-sâng'a *or* Kô-nâm'a.	Kô-sâng'a *or* Kô-nâm'a.	
Black, *a.*	Yâ'kâ.	Yâ'kâ.	
Bladder, *n.*	Pûm'shûr.	Pûm'shûr.	
Blind (wholly), *a.*	Mîg-lû'a.	Mîg lû'a.	
Blind (partially), *a.*	Mî-kê'a.	Mî-kê'a.	

Blood, *n.*	Î *or* î'yê.	Î *or* î'yê.	
Blow, *v.*	Mût	Mût.	
Board, *n.*	Si'pâng.	Si'pâng,	
Boat, *n.*	È'lûng.	Et'kûng *or* Ê'lûng.	
Bow of ditto, *n.*	Kû'dûm.	Kû'dûm.	
Stern of ditto, *n.*	Kûn'kông.	Kûn'kông.	
Bail water out of ditto, *v.*	Â'sî kâ'buin.	Â'sî kâ'buin.	
Paddle ditto, *v.*	Dû.	Dû.	
Pole ditto, *a.*	Sân.	Sân.	
Bamboo boiler for ditto, *n.*	Pê'jûk.	Pê'jûk.	
Body, *n.*	Â'muir.	Â'muir.	
Boil water, *v. i.*	Û'sâ mô.	Û'sâ mô.	
Warm ditto, *v.*	A'sî si'gû kîr.	Â'sî si'gû kîr.	
Bone, *n.*	Â'lông.	A'lông.	Shin-bone=lê'lông (â'lê=leg.) Backbone=gîr'jî â'lông. Forearm-bone=lâk'lông (â'lâk=arn.) Breast-bone=kur'lông. Rib=dôr'lông. Jaw-bone=sog'lông.
Borrow, *v.*	Nâr.	Nâr.	
Both of us, *a. a. pro.*	Ngâ'nyî.	Ngâ'nyî.	(Lit., ngâ=I, nyî=two.)
Both of you, *a. a. pro.*	Nâ'nyî.	Nâ'nyî.	(Lit., nâ=you, nyî=two.)
Both of them, *a. pro.*	Bû'nyî.	Bû'nyî.	(Lit., bû=first syllable of bûlû=they, and nyi=two.)
Bough, *n.*	Â'gleng.	Â'gleng.	
Bow, *n.*	Î.	Î.	I can detect no difference between this word and the one for *blood*.
Boy, *n.*	Kô mî'lông.	Kô mî'lông.	(Lit., kô=child, mîlông=male.)
Bracelet (silver), *n.*	Kôn'gê.	Kôn'gê.	Those made by our Mooryas of silver.
(brass), *n.*	Kâ'pûng.	Kâ'pûng.	Those made by Abor braziers.

English.	Shai-yâng Miri.	Abor.	Remarks.
Brain, *n.*	Pin'yâ.	Pin'yâ.	
Break, *v.*	Miris have no general word for break (tîr-tû'to-kâ=break wood by hand).		
Break wind, *v.*	Yêpü pê.	Yêpü pê.	
Breast, *n.*	Ân'yŭk.	Ân'yŭk.	
Nipple, *n.*	Nyûk'pî.	Nyûk'pî.	
Breath, *n.*	Ngâ.	Ngâ.	
Breathe, *v.*	Ngâ.	Ngâ.	
Bridge, *n.*	É'gâ.	É'gâ.	
Bring, *v.*	Bôm-â-lângkâ.	Bôm-â-lângkâ.	If article is in possession of party asked to bring it.
Bring (fetch), *v.*	Lâ-to-kâ'kâ.	Lâ-to-kâ'kâ.	The *imperative* causal added to "lâ"=take, bring.
Brother, *n.*	Bui'râ.	Bui'râ.	
Do., eldest.	Yai.	Bu'ibuing.	When called.
Do., youngest.	Called by name.	Called by name.	
Brother-in-law.	Mâk'bô *or* yî'gâ.	Mâk'bô *or* yî'gâ.	If wife's brother is older than wife, he is called "mâk'bô" by wife's husband, if younger, yî'gâ; and "similarly" wife's brother, if older than her, calls her husband "yî'gâ," and if younger "mâk'bô." If husband is older than wife's brother, and the latter older than his sister, both brothers-in-law call one another mâk'bô."
Broom, *n.*	Sâm'puk.	Sâm'puk.	
Buffalo, *n.*	Men'jâk.	Men'jâk.	

Build, house, *v.*	Êkûm mô.	Êkûm mô.	Lit., ê-kûm=house, mô=make.
Burn, or destroy with fire, *v.*	U-mü'lâ rôm-pâk.	....	
Burn (with ditto), *v.*	Ûmü bâ.	Ûmü bâ.	
Bury, *v.*	Yû.	Yû.	
Busy, *a.*	Mâ-mâng'a.	Mâ-mâng'a.	Lit., no leisure (mâ=leisure).
Buttock (rump), *n.*	Kô-pî'ang.	Kô-pî'ang.	
But,* *conj.*	Bê'ang.	Bê'ang.	* Butt, *n.*, jâmlûm (end limit.)
Buy, *v.*	Re.	Re.	
Calf of leg, *n.*	Lê'pûm.	Lê'pûm.	
Call, *v.*	Gok.	Gok.	
Cane, *n.*	Jê'ing.	Jê'ing.	*Three kinds.* Assamese. Miri. Raidâng=rai'dâng. Bêt gâz=tai'ô. Jâtî gaz=yô'tûng.
Cannot do.	Î-lâ'mâ.	Î-lâ'mâ.	(î=root of verb to do, "lâ"=potential mood suffix, and mâ=negative particle).
Carefully, *adv.*	Kâ-shû'lâ.	Kâ-shû'lâ.	(Lit., personally seeing).
Carry child on back, *v.*	Bui.	Bui.	
Carry child on hip, *v.*	Keb-bôm-shû.	....	
Carry basket, bamboo, water, &c, *v.*	Jâ-bôm.	Jâ-bôm.	
Castor-oil plant, *n.*	Tâ'pûm ur'sing.	Tâ'pûm ur'sing.	(Lit., maggot tree.)
Castrate, *v.*	Et'tûm mô.	Et'tûm mo.	The operation is performed by cutting, so why "môto-kâ" is used instead of "gâtto-kâ" it is not easy to say.
Cat, *n.*	Men-dâ'rî.	Men-dâ'rî.	
Catarrh, *n.*	Sâg'rê.	Sâg'rê.	
Catch *v.*	Gâk.	Gâk.	
Catch fish with net, *v.*	Ur'sâp kû.	Ur'sâp kû.	(Ursâp=net.)

English.	Shai-yâng Miri.	Abor.	Remarks.
Catch fish, *v.*, with a bamboo thing called "pôlông" by Assamese.	Jû'rkî nik.	Jû'rkî nik.	(Nik=prod, prick, &c.)
Catch fish, *v.*, with hands in mud.	Ên'gâ ûm.	Ên'gâ ûm.	
Catch fish, *v.*, with rod and line.	Ba-rô'kî kû.	Ba-rô'kî kü.	
Caterpillar, *n.*	Tai'ôp.	Tai'ôp.	
Certainly, chaff, *adv.*	Be-rok'pü.	Be-rok'pu.	
Change, *v.*	Lik-shû.	Lik-shû.	
Chest, *n.*	Âng'keng.	Âng'keng.	
Child, *n.*	Kô.	Kô.	
Chillies, *n.*	Mur'chî.	Mur'chî.	
Chin, *n.*	Sok'kôr.	Sok'kôr.	
Cholera, *n.*	Kî'lî.	Kî'lî.	
"Chudder," worn by women, *n.*	Gâ'sôr.	Gâ'sôr.	
Cinder, *n.* (wood)	Mê'kol.	Mê'kol.	
Clean, *a.*	Nâ-reng'a.	Nâ-reng'a.	(Lit., clear. Clean would be more correctly rendered by "koiâng kâ mâ"=dirt exists not).
Climb hill, get up into house or tree, *v.*	Rô-shâ.	Rê-shâ.	
Cloud, *n.*	Dâ'muir.	Dâ'muir.	
Clap hands, *v.*	Yâ'pâ pi.	Yâ pâ pî.	

Cloudy, *a.*	Dâ-mûm'a.	Dâ-mûm'a.	
Cold (not hot), *a.*	Sî-kîr'a.	Sî-kîr'a.	
Cold season, *n.*	Dîg'in.	Dîg'in.	
Coarse, *a.*	Bî-sâm'a.	Bî-sâm'a.	Also means close together, thick as the dhan has been sown very thickly.
Fine, *a.*	Bâsôr'a.	Bâ-sôr'a.	
Cockroach, *n.*	Tâk'shî.	Tâk'shî.	
Cobweb, *n.*	Rûm'shôr.	Rûm'shôr.	
Collect, *v.*	Lâng-kûm	Lâng-kûm.	
Come, *v.*	Gi'â.	Gi'â.	Root of verb (a compound one,) "gî"=go, "â"=enter.
Come back, *v.*	Gî'lât.	Gî'lât.	"lât" is a particle denoting return.
Comb, *n.*	Tâ'bâp.	Tâ'bâp.	
Comb hair, *v.*	Tûp-shû.	Tûp-shû.	
Commence.	No word. Generally made by using the particle "vô," as— I will commence (doing it)=" Ngâ î-pü'vô". When will you commence work?=" Nâ a-dî'lô â'gîr î-yê-vô'na?		
Common (" chupri"), *n.*	Bôg'râng.	Bôg'râng.	
Companion, *n.*	Â'jon.	Â'jon.	Yûp'jon=sleeping companion. Gi'jon=journey ditto. Kî'jon=sick ditto.
Compensation, *n.*	Â'ra.	Â'ra.	
Condiment, *n.*	Dâ'mui.	Dâ'mui.	Accompaniment to rice. Abors call salt "lô'mui" (â'lô meaning salt).
Consult oracle, *v.*	Tâ'gîr kâ.	Tâ'gîr kâ.	
Cool, *a.*	Ân-ching'a.	Ân-ching'a.	
Cook rice, *v.*	Â'pin mô.	Â'pin mô.	
Cook vegetables, *v.*	Ô'ying kur.	Ô'ying kur.	

English.	Shai'yâng Miri.	Abor.	Remarks.
Cooked (not raw).	Nû'na.	Nû'na.	The "na" is merely an adjectival affix, used, as a rule, when the adjective is combined directly with the noun it qualifies.
Copulate, *v.*	Yo.	Yo.	
Corner, *n.*	Ken'yûng.	Ken'yûng.	
Correct, *a.*	Bê-rok'a.	Bê-rok'a.	Generally used with substantive verb "dâk," or abbreviated form "dâ."
Cotton (from sown plant), *n.*	Shî'pâk.	Shî'pâk.	
Cotton (from cotton tree), *n.*	Gî'mûr.	Gî'mûr.	The cotton tree is called "sing'gî." Miris and Abors use this cotton largely for making pillows.
Cousin, *n.*	Bui'râ kûm'shû.	Bui'râ kûm'shû.	
Count, *v.*	Kî-kî *or* Sân-kî.	Kî-kî, *or* Sân-kî.	
Cover (any article), *v.*	Tâk-kôm.	Tâk-kôm.	
Cover (human being), *v.*	Pô-lik.	Î-lik.	
Cricket, *n.*	Kôm'shêr.	Kôm'shêr.	
Crow, *n.*	Pui'âk.	Pui'âk.	Âg'dî=crow. Â'grâ=raven. Pui'âk=common name for both.
Cockcrow, *v.*	Pa'rôk kôg-nâm'a.	Parôk kôg-nâm'a.	The root of the verb to crow is "kôk," *g* is substituted for *k* for sake of euphony.
Crooked, *a.*	Gur-nâm'a.	Gur-nâm'a.	
Cross, river, *v.*	Â'sî kâ.	Âsî kâ.	
Cry, *v.*	Kâp.	Kâp.	

Cubit, *n.*	Lâg'dû	Lâg'dû.	
Cucumber, *n*,	Mâ'kûng.	Mâ'kûng.	
Custom, *n.*	Î-kâm'a.	Î-kâm'a.	
Cut wood, *v.*	Tâ.	Tâ.	Spilt wood = tâk'to-kâ. Fell a tree = tê'to-kâ.
Cut rice *v.*	Gât.	Gât.	Gâtto-kâ means to cut with a drawing motion, and pâto-kâ to ditto with a striking ditto.
Cut jungle, *v.*	Pâ.	Pâ.	
Cymbal, *n.*	Lû'pi.	Lû'pi.	
Dance, *v.*	Mâk'shâ shâ.	Mâk'shâ shâ.	
Dark (not light), *a.*	Kê-mô'a.	Kê-mô'a.	
Daughter, *n.*	Ô'ma.	Ô'ma.	
Daughter-in-law, *n.*	Yâ'mang.	Yâ'mang.	
Dawn, *a.*	Rô-kôm'a.	Rô-kôm'a.	
Day, *n.*	Lông.	Lông.	
To-day, *n.*	Sì'lô.	Sì'lô.	Lit., "si' = this, "lô" = day.
Yesterday, *n.*	Ma'lô.	Ma'lô.	
Day before ditto *n.*	Kon'nô.	Kon'nô.	
Day before that again, *n.*	Kon'kê.	Kon kê.	
Daylight, *a.*	Pui-âng'a.	Pui-âng'a.	
Dead, *a.*	Sî-kâ'vô.	Sî-kâ'vô.	
Death, *n.*	Sì'nâm.	Sì'nâm.	
Deaf, *a.*	Rû-bê'a.	Ru-bê'a.	
Deal, *v.*	Ka'rêt mô.	Karêt mô two words *viz.*, ka'ret and mô.	
Dear.	No word.		Instead of saying "rice is dear," Miris would say "I am not able to buy." (Assam. "fûslau").
Debt, *n.*	Â'jeng.	Â'jeng.	
Deceive, *v.*	Yât.	Yât,	
Deep (water) *a.*	A-ring'a *or* A-ring'a.	A-ring'a *or* Â-ring'a.	

English.	Shai'yâng.	Abor.	Remarks.
Shallow (water), *a.*	A-ted'a *or* Å-ted'a.	A-ted'a *or* Å-ted'a.	
Deer, *n.*	Si'mon.	Si'mon.	*Assamese.* — *Miri.* hôr-pô ....shî'shûk. ho-rînâ.........dûm'shûng. u-gôrî.........sî'dûm (barking-deer).
Desire (wish), *a.*	Mui.	Mui.	
Dew, *n.*	Nâng'âr.	Nâng'âr.	
Different, *a.*	Âng-û'a.	Âng-û'a.	
Same (alike), *a.*	Â-kâm'a.	Â-kâm'a.	
Die, *v.*	Sît.	Sît.	
Dig (a field) *v.*	Lik.	Lik.	Miris do not really dig, merely scrape the earth about.
Digest food, *v.*	Jen-mô.	Jen-mô.	
Dirty, *a.*	Koi-âng'a.	Ko-âng'a.	
Dismiss (or leave a thing anywhere), *v.*	Mê-pâk.	Mê-pâk.	
Distribute, *v.*	Å-shû.	Å-shû.	
Dive, *v.*	Lûm *or* Dûr-jî.	Lûm *or* Dûr-jî.	
Dog, *n.*	Ê'kî.	Ê'kî.	
Do, *v.*	Î.	Î.	
Door, *n.*	E'âp *or* yâb'gô.	E'âp *or* yâb'gô	
Down stream.	Sok'kô *or* sok'kwa.	Sok'kô *or* sok'kwa	
Up ditto.	Lin'gin.	Lin'gin.	
Dream, *v.*	Mân'ying mâ.	Mân'ying mâ.	

Drink, *v.*	Tu.	Tu.	
Drive (cattle), *v.*	Gâ-len.	Gâ-len.	Drive cattle about slowly, as a herdsman does.
Drum, *n.*	Dûm'dûm.	Dûm'dûm.	Used when dancing.
Dry (mop up), *v.*	Pû-tîr.	Pû-tîr.	
Dry clothes, &c., in sun, *v.*	Lo *or* Lâ.	Lo *or* Lâ.	
Dry " by fire, *v.*	Âm-pui.	Âm-pui.	
Dry fish or meat, *v.*	Â-sân.	Â-sân.	(Over a fire).
Dried fish.	Ngâ'sân.	Ngâ'sân.	(Êngâ=fish).
Dried meat.	Din'sân.	Din'sân.	(Âdin=meat).
Dry wood.	Ur'sing sân'na *or* Å'na.	Ur'sing sân'na *or* Å'na.	The "na" is the same as the "na" noticed opposite "nûna."
Wet "	Ur'sing î-tê'na *or* Å'mâ.	Ur'sing î-tê'na *or* Å'mâ.	Âmâ=dry not, "mâ" being negative particle.
Duck, *n.*	Pa'jâp.	Pa'jâp.	
Dumb, *a.*	Mî-dê'a.	Mî-dê'a.	
Dung, *n.*	Tai.	Tai.	
Dust, *n.*	Pêr'mûk.	Pêr'mûk.	
Dwarf, *n.*	Mî'pet.	Mî'pet.	
Ear, *n.*	Yê'rûng.	Yê'rûng.	
Earring, *n.*	Ken'tû.	Ken'tû *or* ê'tûng.	"Kentû" is the silver one made by the Assamese; êtung is a hollowed bamboo.
Earth, *n.*	Â'mông *or* kê'dê.	Â'mông *or* kê'dê.	
Earthquake, *n.*	Tâ-rô-mô'ton.		
Earthen vessel, *n.*	Kî'ling*	Kî'ling* Dû'pû.	(Kôlsî)* "dûpû" is made locally of bamboo.
Eat, *v.*	Dâ.	Dâ.	
Egg, *n.*	Â'pui	Â'pui.	Yolk of egg="puimôr," white of egg="âsik" (lit., skin).
Eight, *a.*	Pui'nyî.	Pui'nyî.	
Elbow, *n.*	Lâg-gû'lûng.	Lâg-gû'lûng.	

English.	Shai'yâng Miri.	Abor.	Remarks.
Eldest, *a.*	Â-bui-âng'a.	Â-bui-âng'a.	
Elephant, *n.*	Sî'tê, sî'tâ.	Sî'tâ.	
Emerge, *v.*	Len.	Len.	
Empty, *a.*	Âng-â-râng'a.	Âng-â-râng'a.	
Empty house.	Mê-pâk'nâm ê'kûm.	Mê-pâk'nâm ê'kûm.	(Lit., deserted).
Enough.	Puing-kâ'vô.	Puing-kâ'vô.	
Enter, *v.*	Â.	Â.	
Every day, *adv*,	Lâ-dî'pü.	Lâ-dî'pü.	
Everywhere, *adv.*	Â-pui'lâ.	Â-pui'lâ.	
Evening, *n*,	Yŭ'ma.	Yŭ'ma.	
Excrement, *n*,	Tai.	Tai.	
Expel (drive out), *v.*	Men *or* men-pâk.	Men *or* men-pâk.	
Expiate, *v.*	Ú-dâr.	Ú-dâr.	
Explain, *v*,	Lû-bî.	Pô-bî.	
Extinguish fire, *v.*	Mô-mit.	Mô-mit.	
Eye, *n*,	Â'mîk.	Â'mîk.	
Eyelash, *n.*	Mik'shâp.	Mik'shâp.	
Eyebrow, *n.*	Ming'wit.	Ming'wit.	
Face, *n.*	Ming'mô.	Ming'mô.	
Fair, *a.*	Yê-sing'a.	Yê-sing'a.	
Fall, *v.*	O-let.	O-let.	
False, *a.*	Mai-nâm'a.	Mai-nâm'a.	

Father, *n.*	Bâ'bû.	**Bâ'bû.**	When an outsider asks a question about anyone's father, he alludes to him as "âbû."
Father-in-law, *n.*	**Kâ'kî.**	**Kâ'kî.**	
Far, *a.*	**Mô-teng'a.**	Mô-teng'a.	
Fast (quickly), *adv.*	Mai-nâ'pü.	Mai-nâ'pü.	
Fathom, *n.*	Bôm'yâm.	Bôm'yâm.	
Fat (person).	Âmuir bâ-tê-rû'dâk.	**Âmuir bâ-tê-rû'dâk**	Lit. "body large very is." It is against custom to talk of a *fat* person or child.
Fat (animal), *a.*	Jî-nâm'a.	Jî-nâm'a.	
Fear, *a.*	Pê'shâ.	Pê'shâ.	
Feather, *n.*	Âm'wit.	Âm'wit.	Same word as for hair?
Female, *n.*	Mî'ma.	Mî'ma.	
Female organ, *n.*	Î'tü.	Î'tü.	
Fence, *n.*	Ê'tôr.	Ê'tôr.	A very substantial one, made with logs of wood.
Fetch, *v.*	Made by root of verb "lâ"=take, bring, and the causal "kâ" inserted between the imperative to'kâ, as "lâ-tô-kâ'kâ."		
Few, *a.*	Â'kâ â'nyî.	Â'kâ â'nyî.	Lit., one, two (Assam. "dûi êtâ").
Fie! *ex.*	Tât'kyê. / Kâng'kyê.	Tât'kyê. / Kâng'kyê.	(tâtkyî"=fie! to anything *said*. "tât"=*hear*, "kângkyê" fie! to anything *seen*; kâ=root of verb *to see*).
Field, *n.*	Â'rig.	Â'rig.	
Fight, *v.*	Pâ-muin-shû.	Pâ-muin-shû.	
Fill (a boat, basket, &c.), *v.*	Reb-lik.	Reb-lik.	
Finger, *n.*	Lâk'keng.	Lâk'keng.	
Finish, *v.*	No word. **Made by using** completive particles "in" and "vô," as—I will finish weaving to-morrow="yâmpô shûm-in-yê'pü," I have finished doing it="ngâ î-in-tô'vô."		
Fire, *n.*	U'mü.	U'mü.	
Fire-place, *n.*	Mê'rôm.	Mê'rôm.	
Fire gun (or bow) *v.*	Âp.	Âp.	

English.	Shai'yâng Miri.	Abor.	Remarks.
Fish, *n.*	Êng'â.	Êng'â.	*Names of a few fish.* English. Assamese. Miri. Mahseer... Jûngâ pê-tiâ.. ngâ kû. Go-riâ......... tin'gîr. Ârî .... si'â nâ'reng. Gô-rûâ ...... ngâ'na. Bûkâ .... tâ'gâ. Nê-pûrâ ...... ngâ'pî. Bhângon...... ngâ'rî. Son-dárî ...... or'pê. Al .... ta'lî. Shrimps ... Hing-ôrâ mâs. nâ'reng. Prawns ... Misâ mâs ... ta'shûn. Shark ... Gô-rûâ ...... ngâ'na.*
Fist, *n.*	Lâk'tûm.	Lâk'tûm.	
Five, *a.*	Âng'â.	Pil'ngâ, *or* Âng'â.	
Flame, *n.*	Umû mayô.	Umû mayô.	
Flat, *a.*	Â-jep'a.	Â-jep'a.	
Flea, *n,*	Î'pô	Î'pô.	
Flesh, *n.*	Â'din.	Â'din.	
Flint, striker, *n.*	Shâ'mâk.	Shâ'mâk.	
Float, *v.*	Pû-lem.	Pû-lem.	
Fly, *n.*	Tai'ing.	Tai'ing.	
Gadfly, *n.*	Tai'ûp.	Tai'ûp.	
Firefly, *n.*	Uk'shî mân'ying.	Uk'shî mân'ying.	
Fly, *v.*	Yop.	Yop.	

Flower, *n.*	Â′pûn.	Â′pûn.	
Fog, *n.*	Mûk′shûp.	Mûk′shûp.	
Foot, *n.*	Lê′pô.	Lê′pô.	
Fool, *n.*	Sim′ât.	Si′mât.	
For, *prep.*	Made by particle "pü."	....	For what? "In-kâ′pu?"
Forget *v.*	Mit-pân.	Mitpân.	
Forehead, *n.*	Tûpt′â.	Tûp′tâ.	
Four, *a.*	Â′pî.	Â′pî.	
Fowl, *n.* (tame).	Pa′rôk.	Pa′rôk.	
Cock, *n.*	Rôk′pô.	Rôk′pô.	
Hen, *n.*	Rông′na.	Rông′na.	
Fowl (wild), *n.*	Pa′shin.	Pa′shin.	
Cock, *n.*	Shin′pâ *or* pô.	Shin′pâ *or* pô.	
Hen, *n.*	Shin′na.	Shin′na.	
Frighten (by words), *v.*	Lû-rî.	Lûrî.	
Frighten (by starting out from hiding-place on any one), *v.*	Mô-rît.	Mô-rît.	
Frog, *n.*	Tâ′tuk.	Tâ′tuk.	
From	Made by the postposition "lok" (*vide* Grammar).		
Froth (of liquor), *n.*	Â′pût.	Â′pût.	"Si′pût"=froth (foam) from water, "â′si" =water, "pin′pût"=froth from rice ("â′pui"=cooked rice).
Fruit, *n.*	Â′yê.	Â′yê.	
Get up (from lying or sitting posture) *n.*	Dâ-râp.	Dâ-râp.	
Get up (ladder or hill, &c.) *v.*	Shâ.	Shâ.	
Get down ditto, *v.*	Oi.	Oi.	
Ghat, *n.*	Pui′gâ.	Pui′gâ.	

* *N.B.*—Miris have no separate names for the fish called si′tol, bô-râ′li, î′ling, rô, mî-ri′kâ, jâ′râ mâs, kun-si′yâ (eel), &c., by the Assamese.

English.	Shai'yâng Miri.	Abor.	Remarks.
Ginger, *n.*	Tâ'kê.	Tâ'kê.	
Girl, *n.*	Kô mi'ma.	Kô mi'ma.	Lit., child, female.
Give, *v.*	Bî.	Bî.	
Give back (return), *v.*	Bî-lât.	Bî-lât.	
Go, *v.*	Gî.	Gî.	
Goat, *n.*	Shâ'ben.	Shâ'ben.	
Goitre, *n.*	Lü'pû *or* gû'pû.	Lü'pû *or* gû'pû.	
Grandfather, *n.*	Tâ'tô.	Tâ'tô.	
Grandmother, *n.*	Yai'ô *or* yai'yô.	Yai'ô *or* yai'yô.	
Grandson, *n.*	Nâ'tî.*	... .	* Assam. Miris have no word.
Granddaughter, *n.*	Nâ'tî.*	....	
Granary, *n.*	Kem'shûng.	Kem'shûng.	
Grasshopper	Tâ'kôm.	Tâ'kôm.	
Grave, *n.*	Â'gô.	Â'gô.	
Green, *a.*	Yâ-gê'a.	Yâ-gê'a.	
Grey hair.	Dûmpû.	Dûm'pû.	
Groin, *n.*	Âr'kep.	Âr'kep.	
Gum, *n.*	Î'lê.	Î'lê.	Itch, *n.*=Â'bûk.
Gun, *n.*	Âb'bûk.	Âb'bûk.	
Hair (of head), *n.*	Dûm'wit.	Dûm'wit.	
Hair (of arms), *n.*	Lâng'wit.	Lâng'wit.	
Hair (of legs), *n.*	Lem'wit.	Lem'wit.	
Hair (of chest), *n.*	Kurm'wit.	Kurm'wit.	
Half, *n.*	Kê'kon.	Kê'kon.	
Half way, *a.* (midway).	Râ-dâ'lâ *or* Pong kok.	Râ-dâ'lâ *or* Pong'kok.	(Râ'dâng=middle, lâ=in.)
Hand, *n.*	Lâk'pô.	Lak'pô.	

Hang up, *v.*	Tû-shâ.	Tû-shâ.	Suspend a thing is "pâk-puit'to-kâ."
Happy, *a.*	Û'gu.	Û'gu.	Assamese word, but Miris use no other.
Hard, *a.*	Tol'dô.	Tol'dô.	
Hat, *n.*	Dûm'lûp.	Dûm'lûp.	
Hatchet, *n.*	Ê'gin.	Ê'gin.	
Hawk, *n.*	’na.	Ê'na.	Assamese word.
He, *pron.*	Bui.	Bui.	
Head, *n.*	Tûk'kû *or* Dûm'pông.	Tûk'kû *or* Dûm'pông.	
Headache, *n.*	Dûm'pô mû-nâm'a.	Dûm'pô mû-nâm'a.	
Heart, *n.*	Âng.	Âng.	
Help, *v.*	No word. Made by use of particle "dûm," as—Help me to do it, "Ngôm î-dûm-shû-îkâ."		
Here, *adv.*	Sâ'pü.	Sâ'pü.	
Hiccup, *n.*	Ja'kuk.	Ja'kuk.	
Hide, *v.*	Lur-shû.	Lur-shû.	
High, *a.*	Bâ-dông'a *or* ô-id'a.	Bâ-dông'a *or* ô-id'a.	
Hill, *n.*	Â'dî.	Â'dî.	
Him, *pron.*	Buim.	Buim.	
Hip, *n.*	Û'ging.	Û'ging.	
Hoe, *n.*	Kû'yâp.	Kû'yâp.	
Hole, *n.*	Â'rûng.	Â'rûng.	
Honey, *n.*	Tân'gût â'lông.	Tâng'ût â'lông.	
Honeycomb, *n.*	Tân'gût â'kâng.	Tâng'ût â'kâng.	
Horn, *n.*	Â'reng.	Â'reng.	
Hot (from sun), *a.*	In-nâm'a.	In-nâm'a.	
Hot (from fire), *a.*	Pâm'kyê.	Pâm'kyê.	
Hot, rice, water, &c., &c., *a.*	Gû-nâm'a.	Gû-nâm'a.	
Hot season, *a.*	Dî'yŭ.	Dî'yŭ.	
House, *n.*	È'kûm.	Ê'kûm.	
Wall of ditto, *n.*	Bâ'rê.	Bâ'rê.	
Front of ditto, *n.*	Gê'dâng.	Gê'dâng.	

English.	Shai'yâng Miri.	Abor.	Remarks.
Roof of house, *n.*	Â'kâp.	Â'kâp.	
Back of ditto *n.*	Yâp'kûr.	Yâp'kûr.	
How many	A-dit'kâ.	A-dit'kâ.	
Hump-backed, *a.*	Pû-gît'a *or* Tûng-gîr'a.	Pû-gît'a *or* Tûng-gîr'a.	
Hundred, *a.*	Ling'kâ.	Ling'kâ.	
Hungry, *a.*	Kê-nông'a.	Kê-nông'a.	
Husk rice, *v.*	Dâ'nâm î.	Dâ'nâm î.	
Husband, *n.*	Mî'lô.	Mî'lô.	
Hypocrite, *n.*			
I, *pron.*	Ngâ.	Ngâ.	
Ill, *a.*	Kî-nâm'a.	Kî-nâm'a.	
In, *prep.*	Made by a post	position "lâ".	
Incubate, *v.*	Gûm-mô.		
Indian-corn, *n.*	Sê'pâ.	Sê'pâ.	
Inside, *n.*	Â'râng.	Â'râng.	
Instantly, *adv.*	Lê-têr-kâ-pü.	Lê-têr-kâpü.	
Iron, *n.*	Yôk'din.	Yôk'din	
Itch, *n.*	Tai'ôt.		
Ivory, *n.*	Sî'tê ta'reng	Sî'tê ta'reng.	
Jack-fruit, *n.*	Bwel'lâng.	Bwel'lâng.	
Jack-tree, *n.*	Bwel'lâng ur'sing.	Bwel'lâng ur'sing.	
Jacket, *n.*	Men-sâ'ron.	Men-sâ'ron.	
Jackal, *n.*	Gâ'lûk.	Gâ'lûk.	Assamese "shô'lâ."
Juice (of fruit), *n.*	Â'lâng.	Â'lâng.	Sap (from trees)=â'bâg.

Jump, *v.*	Shûm *or* shûm-kî.	Shûm *or* shûmkî.	This verb is usually used in conjunction with the root verb "kâ"=cross over anything, as "jump that"="dem shûm-kâto-kâ."
Jungle, *n.*	Yŭm'râng.	Yŭm'rang.	
Keep, *v.*	Ma-shî.	Ma-shî.	
Kick, *v.*	Tû.	Tû.	
Kill, *v.*	Mô-kê.	Mô-kê.	
King, *n.*	Mî'gôm.	Mî'gôm.	
Kiss, *v.*	Dâ-shûk.	Dâ-shûk.	
Knee, *n.*	Lê'buing.	Lê'buing.	
Kneel, *v.*	Lê'buing kô-nî.	Lê'buing kô-nî.	
Knife, *n.*	Yôk'shîk.	Yôk'shîk.	
Handle of do., *n.*	Yôg'lê.	Yôg'lê.	
Blade of do., *n.*	Âr.	Âr.	
Sharpen do., *v.*	Pui-rât *or* pui.	Pui-rât *or* pui.	
Dao, *n.*	Mât'shîk.	Mât'shîk.	Really a large heavy knife.
Knot, *n.*	Rî'êk.	Rî'êk.	Tied in string, cane, bark of tree, &c. To tie up a thing in the corner of one's cloth is "pai-êkto-kâ."
Know (understand), *v.*	Ken.	Ken.	
Labour (work), *n.*	Â'gêr.	Â'gêr.	
Labour, *v.*	Â'gêr î.	Â'gêr î.	
Ladder, *n.*	Kô'bâng.	Kô'bâng.	Really a notched piece of wood used to ascend and descend a house.
Lame, *a.*	Lê-vê'a.	Lê-vê'a.	
Language, *n.*	Â'gôm.	Â'gôm.	
Large, *a.*	Bâ-tê'a.	Bâ-tê'a.	
Last, *a.*	Mê-lâm'a.	Mê-lam'a.	
Last year, *a.*	Mon'ying.	Mon'ying.	
Last moon (or month), *a.*	Sî'na pô'lô.	Sî'na pô'lô.	Lit., dead moon.
Late.	Ngâk.	Ngâk.	

English.	Shai'yâng Miri.	Abor.	Remarks.
Laugh, *v.*	Yîr *or* nyîl.	Yîr *or* nyîl.	
Laughable, *a.*	Yîr-ling'a.	Yîr-ling'a, *or* nyîl-ling'a.	
Lay egg, *v.*	Âpui pui.	Âpui pui.	
Lazy, *a.*	Bôm-râm'a, *or* lâ-bâg'a.	Bôm-râm'a, *or* lâ-bâg'a.	
Leach, *n.*	Tâ'pât.	Tâ'pât.	
Leaf, *n.*	Ur'sing ân'na.	Ur'sing â'nna.	
Leaf (large, used to eat off), *n.*	Ek'kâm.	Ek'kâm.	
Leak, *v.*	Dâ'dî ô.	Dâ'dî ô.	Only applicable to a leak from above. "The boat is leaking" would be— ê-lû'lâ â'sî â'dûng. boat in water entering is.
Leisure, *n.*	Mâ.	Mâ.	
Leg, *n.*	Â'lê.	Â'lê.	
Leopard, *n.*	Tâ'kâr.	Tâ'kâr.	
Let go, *v.*	Mê-lek.	Mê-lek.	
Lick, *v.*	Yâk.	Yâk.	
Lie down, *v.*	Ket.	Ket.	
Lift, *v.*	Jâ-shâ.	Jâ-shâ.	
Light (in weight), *a.*	Ê-châng'a.	Ê-châng'a.	
Light fire, *v.*	U'mü pâr.	U'mü pâr.	
Lightning, *n.*	Yâ'rî.	Yâ'rî.	
Like, *a.* (noting resemblance).	Kê'shâ.	Kê'shâ.	Nâ sîmât kêshâ } =you are like a fool. You fool like. } But "you look like an old woman," is— Nom ur-jâ'pü kâ'dâ.

Liquor, *n.*	Â'pông.	Â'pông.	Two kinds are made, called "na'gin" and "pô'rô." They are both made from rice, though the latter ("pô'rô") is often made of Indian-corn, "ân'yât," a sort of Job's-tears, and various other grains, and the process of manufacturing them is slightly different. After the rice has been boiled, it is well mixed with a quantity of charred *dhan* husk, after which some carefully and wondrously prepared yeast is added, and the whole is then tied up in large leaves and kept so for ten days, or even as long as a month.
Listen, *v.*	Tât.	Tât.	
Little (small), *a.*	Â-mê'a. Ân-jâ'a.	Â-mê'a. Ân-jâ'a.	
Little (quantity), *n.*	Ân-jâ'kâ.	Ân-jâ'kâ.	
Liver, *n.*	Âin.	Âin.	
Load, *n.*	Ju'rîk.	Ju'rîk.	
Loin, *n.*	Û'ging.	Û'ging.	(Includes waist too).
Lonesome, *a.*	Rông-âm'a.	Rông-âm'a.	
Long (in length), *a.*	Bâ-dông'a.	Bâ-dông'a.	
Look, *v.*	Kâ.	Kâ.	
Loom, *n.*	Gê'gûr.	Gê'gûr.	
Loose (not tight), *a.*	É-rôk'a.	É-rôk'a.	
Loosen, *v.*	Ê'rôk mô.	Ê'rôk mô.	
Louse, *n.*	Tüg.	Tüg.	Most Miris say "taïk."
Low ground.	Jî'kông.	Jî'kông.	
Mad, *n.*	Sî'mât.	Sî'mât.	(Lit. fool).
Maggot, *n.*	Tâ'pûm.	Tâ'pûm.	
Make, *v.*	No *general* word like in English, or Assamese.		
Male organ, *n.*	È'mâk.	[illegible]m'âk.	
Man, *n.*	Mî'lông.	Mî'lông.	
Many, *a.*	Bâ'jê.	Bâ'jê.	
Marry, *v.*	Yâm'na mô, *or* lâto-kâ=take in marriage. Yâm'na tât=ask in marriage.		

English.	Shai'yâng Miri.	Abor.	Remarks.
Master (owner), *n.*	Rû'tûm.	Rû'tûm.	
Mat, *n.*	Em'pû.	Em'pû.	
Matikalai, *n.*	Rêr'râ.	Rêr'râ.	
Matter (pus), *n.*	Tâ'shût.	Tâ'shût.	
Measure, *v.*	Miris have no general word. They measure by— fathoms, | cubits, | spans, | and fingers. bôm'yâm. | lâg'dû. | pin'gôp. | lâk'kê pâ'tân. so, if anything has to be measured they would say— fathom (it)=bôm'yâm yâm-kî'to-kâ ("kî"=count), or cubit (it)=lâg'dû dû-kî'to-kâ. or span (it)=pin'gôp gôp-kî'to-kâ.		
Medicine, *n.*	Sin'na.	Sin'na.	Jungly herbs, &c.
Melt, *v.*	Jin-mô.	Jin-mô.	
Micturate, *v.*	Asî sî.	Asî sî.	
Midday, *n.*	Lô-in-kâ'vô.	Lô-in-kâ'vô.	
Midnight, *n.*	Yô'râng kî-shû-pâ'gê.	Yô'râng kî-shû-pâ'gê.	
Mine, *pron.*	Ngâ'ka.	Ngâ'ka.	Poss. case of personal pronoun "Ngâ"=I.
Miscarriage, *n.*	Ô'rî.	Ô'rî.	She has had a miscarriage is "Bui au ô-rî'tô."
Mist.	*See* "Fog."		
Mistake, *v.*	This word is made by using a particle "mûr," signifying mistake, as— Ngâ î-mûr-shû'tô / I did mistake have } I did (it) by mistake.		

Mithon, *n.*	Ur'sâ.	Ur'sâ.	
Mix (rice, "dhan", &c.), *v.*	Yôn-bui-shû.	Yôn-bui-shû.	
Money, *n.*	Mûr'kông.	Mûr'kông.	
Monkey, *n.*	Sî'bê.	Sî'bê.	
Month, or moon, *n.*	Pô'lô.	Pô'lô.	
Moon, full, *n.*	Pô'lô bû'pui.	Pô'lô bû'pui.	
Moon, new, *n.*	Pô'lô â'nŭ.	Pô'lô â'nŭ.	
Moon light, *n.*	Lô-lât'a.	Lô-lât'a.	
More.	Ân-jâ-kâ'tê.	Ân-jâ-kâ'tê.	Lit., little also.
Morning, *n.*	Rô.	Rô.	
Morrow, *n.*	Yâm'pô.	Yâm'pô.	
Day after ditto, *n.*	Rô'ê.	Rô'ê.	
Day after that, *n.*	Rô'kê.	Rô'kê.	
Mosquito, *n.*	Tâ'mît.	Tâ'mît.	
Mother, *n.*	Nâ'na.	Nâ'na.	If a third person talks of her, he or she would say "âna."
Moth, *n.*	Pa'puir.	Pa'puir.	
Mouse, *n.*	Kê'bûng	Kê'bûng.	
Mouth, *n.*	Nâp'pâng.	Nâp'pàng.	
Mouth of river, *n.*	Bôg'gâ.	Bôg'gâ.	
Much, *a.*	Bâ-jê'kâ.	Bâ-jê'kâ.	
Mud, *n.*	Bû'kât.		Assam. word, Miris have no other.
Muscle, *n.*	Ai shâ'pon.	Ai shâ'pon.	
Mustard-plant, *n.*	Pre'tû.	Pre'tû.	
My, *pron.*	Ngâ'ka.	Ngâ'ka.	Poss. case of personal pronoun I="Ngâ."
Nail (finger), *n.*	Lâk'shin.	Lâk'shin.	
Nail (toe), *n.*	Lê'in *or* lê'shin.	Lê'in *or* lê'shin.	
Naked, *a.*	Âng-â-râng'a.	Âng-â-râng'a.	Also means "empty."
Name, *n.*	Â'muin.	Â'muin.	

English.	Shai'yâng Miri.	Abor.	Remarks.
Narrow, *a.*	Tâ-pet'a.	Tâ-pet'a.	
Nasty, *a.*	Bê-lûm'a.	Bê-lûm'a.	
Navel, *n.*	Kîn'yôn.	Kîn'yôn.	
Near, *a.*	Â-nin'a.	Â-nin'a.	
Neck, *n.*	Ling'gûng.	Ling'gûng.	
Necklace, *n.*	Tâ'dôk.	Tâ'dôk.	Made of Abor beads. If made of small imported beads it is called "dôk-shîrî."
Needle, *n.*	Pa'shî.	Pa'shî.	
Neither, *comp. pron.*	Sin *or* tê.	Sin *or* tê.	
Nest, *n.*	Â'shûp. Â'sûp.	Â'shûp. Â'sûp.	
Net, *n.*	Ur'shâp *or* Ur'sâp.	Ur'shâp *or* Ur'sâp.	
Never, *adv.*	A-dî'lô sin mâ.	A-dî'lô sin mâ.	Lit., "when even not."
New, *a.*	Â'nû.	Â'nû.	
Nice sound, *a.*	Tât-pô'a.	Tât-pô'a.	
Night, *n.*	Yâ.	Yâ.	
To-night, *n.*	Sî'yâ.	Sî'yâ.	
Morrow night, *n.*	Yâm'pô yŭm.	Yâm'pô yŭm.	
Night after that, *n.*	Rô'yâ.	Rô'yâ.	
Last night, *n.*	Moi'yâ.	Moi'yâ.	
Night before ditto, *n.*	Kôn'yâ.	Kôn'yâ.	
Night before that, *n.*	Kôn-kê'yâ.	Kôn-kê'yâ.	
Nine, *a.*	Kâ'nâng.	Kâ'nâng.	
Noise, *a.*	Ngôm-nâm'a.	Ngôm-nâm'a.	
None, *a.*	Kâ'mâng.	Kâ'mâng.	
Nose, *n.*	Yê'bûng.	Yê'bûng.	

Nothing, *n.*	Â-tí'kâ sin ka mâ.	Â-tí'kâ sin kâ mâ.	Lit., *anything at all* exists not.
Now, *adv.*	Shû'pâk.	Shû'pâk.	
Nowadays, *adv.*	Sí'lô ma'lô.	Sí'lô ma'lô.	Lit., *this day yesterday* (Assam. "âjê kâli."
Oath.	Pê-shû-nâm'a.	Pê-shû-nâm'a.	
Oil, *n.*	Tûlâng.	Tû'lâng.	
Old (not new), *a.*	Â-kû'a.	Â-kû'a.	
Old man, *n.*	Mû'jing.	Mû'jing.	
Old woman, *n.*	Ur'jâ.	Ur'jâ.	
Once.	Lê-têr'kâ.	Lê-têr'kâ.	
One, *a.*	Têr.	Têr.	
Only, *adv.*	No word, made by particle "â," as, "I only saw one deer." { Ngâ sí-monem â-têr-âkâ kâtô. / I deer one only saw.		
Open (or unfasten) a thing, *v.*	Tâ.	Tâ	
Open door, *v.*	Yâb'gô sí-gê.	Yâb'gô sí-gê.	
Open mouth, *v.*	Nâp'pâ da kô-kâ.	Nâp'pâ da kô-kâ.	(The "da" is a demonstrative pronoun).
Or, *conj.*	No word. Made by particle "yü" tacked on to end of interrogative particle "na;" as, "Will you give (it) or not ?" "Nâ bi-yê-nayü bi-mâ-nayü"? Sometimes the "yu" is omitted altogether, as, "Will you go or not ?" Nâ gí-puiâ gí-pu-mââ ? (*vide* Grammar.)		
Orange, *n.*	Ôm-tí'râng.	Ôm-tí'râng.	
Orphan, *n.*	Ô'pân.	Ô'pân.	Same word as for *poor*. I suppose an orphan is synonymous with poor among Miris.
Otter, *n.*	Sí'râm.	Sí'râm.	
Ought, *v.*	No word. Made by a particle "kân" attached to root of verb, as, "Nâ da-kân-dûai," You ought to eat. / you eat ought.		
Ours (*poss.* of we).	Ngâ-lû'ka	Ngâ-lû'ka.	
Outside, *a.*	Lû-yü'a.	Lû-yü'a.	

English.	Shai'yâng Miri.	Abor.	Remarks.
Own, *a.*	Â-î'ka.	Â-î'ka.	
Paddle, *n.*	Rê bât.	Rê'bât.	
Paddle boat, *v.*	Du.	Du.	
Painful, *a.*	Ding-nâm'a.	Ding-nâm'a.	
Panji, *n.*	Ôr.	Ôr.	
Parrot, *n.*	Pa'bê.	Pa'bê.	
Peacock, *n.*	Tâ'dê.	Tâ'dê.	
Perspiration,	Î-lâm'a.	Î-lâm'a.	
Perhaps, *adv.*	É'sông.	É'sông.	
Person, *n.*	Tâ'nî.	Tâ'nî.	
Petticoat, *n.*	Ê'gê.	Ê'gê.	
Pick nose, *v*	Yê'bûng â-shû.	Yê'bûng âshû.	
Pick leaves, *v.*	Pak.	Pak.	
Pick fruit, *v.*	Puil *or* Pû.	Puil *or* pû.	
Pierce (with spear, bullet, arrow, &c.) *v.*	Tô-pât.	Tô-pât.	
Pig (tame) *n.*	É'ek.	É'ek.	
Pig (wild), *n.*	Sî'râ *or* shî'râ.	Sî'râ *or* shî'râ.	
Pinch, *v.*	In.	In.	
Pith, *n.*	Tâk'pôr.	Tâk'pôr.	Name of tree also from which pith is got.
Plantain, *n.*	Ko'pâk.	Ko'pâk.	
Plate, *n.*	Â'rem.	Â'rem.	
Play, *v.*	Î-mân.	Î-mân.	Lit., *do*, in fun, "î"=do, mân=particle denoting fun, play, &c.
Pleased, *a.*	Â'-seng'a.	....	
Poison, *n.*	Yông'mô.	Yông'mô.	
Point (*i.e.*, apex, tip) *n.*	Jâm'jâ *or* yâm'jâ.	Jâm'jâ *or* yâm'jâ.	

Point (at anything with finger), *v.*	Shût-kân.	Shût-kân.	
Pointed, *a.*	Jâm-jong'a.	Jâm-jong'a.	
Poor, *a.*	Ô-pân'a.	Ô-pân'a.	
Porcupine, *n.*	Bâ'buî.	Bâ'buî.	
Porpoise, *n.*	Pwet-tû-kâ'rî.	Pret-tû-kâ'rî.	
Positively, *adv.*	Â-rô'pü.	Â-rô'pü.	Lit., *truly.*
Pot, for cooking rice in, *n.*	Pa'kî.	Pa'kî.	
Pour out, *v.*	Pui-lik.	Pui-lik.	
Pout (look sullen), *v.*	Bû.	Bû.	
Pretty, *a.*	Kân-kân'a.	Kân-kân'a.	
Prophet, *n.*	Mi'ru.	Mi'ru.	Assam, "dondai.
Pull, *v.*	Shâ.	Shâ.	
Pumpkin, *n.*	Mi'gôm tâ'pâ *and* tâ'pâ pâ'rô.	Mi'gôm tâ'pâ *and* tâ'pâ pâ'rô.	Two kinds "mîgôm"= Râja, called "mî-gôm tâpâ" because eaten by *Sahebs.* It is the common red-looking pumpkin.
Punkah, *n.*	Moi'âp.	Moi'âp.	
Punkah, *v.*	Moi'âp yâp.	Moi'âp yâp.	
Put down (*or* place) anything, *v.*	Ma.	Ma.	
Quarrel, *v.*	Lû-muin-shû.	Lû-muin-shû.	
Quick, *adv.*	Mai-nâ'pü.	Mai-nâ'pü.	
Quilt, *n.*	Gâ'dû.	Gâ'dû.	These quilts are peculiar to this part of the country. They are made by Abors as well as Miris, though the *latter* make the *best.*
Quiver, *n.*	Gâd'bûng.	Gâd bûng.	
Raft, *n.*	Bûr.	Bûr.	
Rain, *n.*	Po'dông.	Po'dông.	

English.	Shai'yâng Miri.	Abor.	Remarks.
Rainbow, *n.*	Lê'bâng *or* Mû'rê.	Lê'bâng.	
Rat, *n.*	Bû'beng.	Bû'beng.	
Rapid, *n.*	Bû'teng.	Bû'teng.	
Raw, *a.*	Î-têng'a.	Î-têng'a.	
Ready, *v.*	No word. Miris have a particle "shî," which, used in conjunction with the root verb "mô," means "*make ready*," as, "make *ready* the boat"="ê-lûng'em mô-shî'to-kâ." The word *ready*, however, is not used as frequently as it is in English. You would not, for instance, say in Miri "get *ready* to go" (anywhere), "Are you *ready*?" &c., &c.		
Reap, *v.*	Gât.	Gât. *Yit.	Cut with a drawing motion. *Really *pick*, Abors pick the ears.
Rear, child, animal, *v.*	Û.	Û.	
Received, *v.*	Pâ-tô'vô.	Pâ-tô'vô.	
Recognise, *v.*	Kâng-ken.	Kâng-ken.	
Red, *a.*	Lü-nâm'a.	Lü-nâm'a.	
Remainder.	Ngân.	Ngân.	
Remain, *v.*	Dû-lâng'kâ.	Dû-lâng'kâ.	
Remind, *v.*	Lû-pâ-lâng'kâ.	Lû-pâ-lâng'kâ.	
Reprisal, *n.*	Lâ'lik.	Lâ'lik.	("Lâ"=take, "lik"=change).
Reside, *v.*	Yê.	Yê.	
Return, *v.*	No word. Made by particle "lât," sometimes used in conjunction with a second particle "kû" (*vide* Grammar).		
Rhinoceros, *n.*	Sâ'rok, *or* Shâ'rok.	Sâ'rok, *or* Shâ'rok.	
Rhinoceros beetle, *n.*	Yapuit.		
Rib, *n.*	Dôr'lông.	Dôr'lông.	

Rice (unhusked), *n.*	Âm.	Âm.	*Different kinds of dhan.* *Assamese.* — *Miri.* Kônî dhân= aiâk. Dûmrâ= dânggûm. Âu= âmrâ. Nâli= âmdâng.
Rice (husked), *n.*	Âm'buin.	Âm'buin.	
Rice (cooked), *n.*	Â'pîn.	Â'pîn.	
Rich, *a.*	Mî-rem'a.	Mî-rem'a.	
Ring-worm, *n.*	Tâ'rûk.	Tâ'rûk.	
Rings of thin strips of bamboo worn by Abors below knee, *n.*	Lê'rûm.	Lê'rûm.	
Ripe, *a.*	Min'na.	Min'na.	
River, *n.*	Â'sî â'bûng.	A'sî â'bûng.	Lit., abounding ("â'bû"=whole) with water.

NAMES OF RIVERS IN VICINITY OF SADIYA.

English.	*Miri and Abor.*
Brahmaputra.	Dê'lô.
Dihong.	Sî'âng.
Dibang.	Sî'kang.
Sisseri.	Sî'sâr.

"Â'sî" is "water" in Miri, but there are many names for rivers which do not commence with "sî."

Road, *n.*	Bê'dâng, *or* Lâm'bü.	Bê'dâng, *or* Lâm'bü.	
Roll up anything, *v.*	Tît.	Tît.	
Root of tree, *n.*	Lê'puir.	Lê'puir.	

English.	Shai'yâng Miri.	Abor.	Remarks.
Rope, *n.*	Shâr'gôk *or* Shâ'rî.	Shâr'gôk *or* Shâ'rî.	"Shârgôk" is the outer bark of the tree called "shârgôk" by Miris, and "shârî" is a creeper.
Rotten (fish, meat, &c.), *a.*	Yâ'na.	Yâ'na.	
Rotten cloth, *a.*	Râm'na.	Râm'na.	
Round, *a.*	Â-pui'a.	Â-pui'a.	
Rub, *v.*	Not *or* Mu r-î.	Not *or* Mur-î.	
Rubber, *n.*	Rôd'bâk.	Rôd bâk.	
Rubber tree.	Ron'na ur'sing.	Ron'na ur'sing.	
Run, *v.*	Dûk.	Dûk.	
Salt, *n.*	Â'lô.	Â'lô.	
Same, *a.*	Âkâm'a	Â-kâm'a.	
Sand, *n.*	Sî'tông. Sul'lî.	Sî'tông. Sul'lî.	"Sullî" is the word in general. "Sîtông" means a large expanse of sand (sandbank).
Say, *v.*	Em.	Em.	
Scar, *n.*	Rê'gông.	Rê'gông.	
Scold, *v.*	Gê.	Gê.	
Scorpion, *n.*	Sê'râ.		
Scratch (as a tiger or cat, &c.) *v.*	Gâ.	Gâ.	
Scratch (as a human being for itch, &c.) *v.*	Ôk	Ôk.	
Scrape, *v.*	Gîd-buin.	Gîd-buin	

Search for, *v.*	Mâ-tâ.	Mâ-tâ.	
Seat, *n.*	Kûng'kê.	Kûng'kê.	Assam. "pîrâ."
See (look), *v.*	Kâ.	Kâ.	
Seize, *v.*	Rôt.	Rôt.	
Sell, *v.*	Ko.	Ko.	
Semen, *n.*	Mâng'nî.	Mâng'nî.	
Send (a message), *v.*	Lû-lik.	Lû-lik.	
Send (a messenger), *v.*	Ma-lik.	Ma-lik.	
Send articles of any sort, *v.*	Bî-lik.	Bî-lik.	
Seven, *a.*	Kî'nit.	Kî'nit.	
Shade of tree, &c., *n.*	Ôg'yŭm or Môg'yŭm.	Ôg'yŭm *or* Môg'yŭm.	
Sadow *n.*	Yâ'lô.	Yâ'lô.	Shadow of human being.
Shake (with fear or rage) *v.*	Jin.	Jin.	
Shake a tree, cloth, &c. *v.*	Tig-buin.	Tig-buin.	
Shallow (water) *a.*	Â-ted'a.	Â-ted'a.	
Shame, *a.*	Ân-ying'a.	Ân-ying'a.	
Shameless, *a.*	Âng-yîr-mâng'a.	Âng-yîr-mâng'a.	
Sharp, *a.*	Rân-nâm'a.	Rân-nâm'a.	
Share, *n.*	Kô'sâg.	Kô'sâg.	
Shave, *v.*	Nâm'mûr î.	Nâm'mûr î.	
Shell, *n.*	Na'tâk.		
Shield, *n.*	Tâm'tê.	Tâm'tê.	
Shoot (with gun or bow) *v.*	Âp.	Âp.	
Short (in stature), *a.*	Ân-deng'a.		
Show, *v.*	Len-kân.	Len-kân.	
Shut door, *v.*	Sik-kâp.	Sik-kâp.	

English.	Shai'yâng Miri.	Abor.	Remarks.
Sick. *a.*	Kî-nâm'a.	Kî-nam'a.	
Sickness, *n.*	Kî.	Kî.	
Sigh, *v.*	Sâ-gî.	Sâ-gî.	
Silently, *adv.*	Â-sô'pü.	Â-sô'pü.	
Similar, *a.*	Â-kâm'a.	Â-kâm'a.	
Similarly, *adv.*	Â-kâm'pü.	Â-kâm'pü.	
Since, *adv.* or *prep.*	No word. Made by particle "rô'sim," as "I have been ill since our dhan was cut." "Ngâ lû'ka âm gâd-rôsim kî'tô.		
Sing, *v.*	Nî'tôm mô.	Nî'tôm mô.	
Singe hair off (pig, &c.) *v.*	Bâ.	Bâ.	
Sister, eldest, *n.*	Buir'ma yai.*	Buir'ma.	* Same as elder brother.
Sister-in-law, *n.*	Mâ'mô *or* ying'na.	Mâ'mô *or* ying'na.	If sister is older that wife "mâ'mô," if younger "yingna;" similarly wife's sisters would call husband's sisters older than themselves "mâ'mô," and if younger "ying'na."
Sit, *v.*	Dû.	Dû.	
Six, *a.*	Kêng.	Kêng.	
Skin, *n.*	Â'sîk.	Â'sîk.	
Skin (an animal), *v.*	Â'sîk dî.	Â'sîk dî.	
Skin (a plantain), *v.*	Kâr.	Kâr.	
Sky, *n.*	Tâ'leng.	Tâ'leng.	
Slave (male), *n.*	Pâk'bâ *or* bô.	Pâk'bâ *or* bô.	
Slave (female), *n.*	Pâng'na.	Pâng'na.	
Sleep, *v.*	Îp, *or* yŭp.	Îp.	

Sleepy, *a.*	Îm-mî'a.	Îm-mî'a.	
	Yŭ-mî'a.		
Slippery, *a.*	Bê-lâb'a.	Bê-lâb'a.	
Slowly, *adv.*	Deng-um'pü.	Deng-um'pü.	
Small (in size), *a.*	Ân-jâ'na.	Ân-jâ'na.	Same "na" as that alluded to at page 13.
Smell (odour), *n.*	Â'rü.	Â'rü.	
Smell, *v.*	Nâm-kî.	Nâm-kî.	
Smoke, *n.*	Ma'kî.	Ma'kî.	
Snag, *n.*	Shü'tûng *and* shü'pông.	Shü'tûng *and* shü'pông.	Trunk of tree, body of ditto.
Snake, *n.*	Tâ'bui.	Tâ'bui.	
Sneeze, *v.*	Âk-shî.	Âk-shî.	
Snore, *v.*	Îm-ngâr, *or* yŭm-ngâr.	Îm-ngâr.	
Snot, *n.*	Yop'shî.	Yop'shî.	
Snow, *n.*	Tû'pâm.	Tû'pâm.	
Soak, *v.*	Pôm.	Pôm.	
Soft (not hard), *a.*	Rê-mâk'a.	Rê-mâk'a.	
Solicit (ask for), *v.*	Kô.	Kô.	
Someone, *n.*	Sê-kô'dî.	Sî-kô'dî.	("Sê'kô"=who, "dî"=particle of vague probability.)
Sometimes, *adv.*	Le'kô, le'kô.	Le'ko, le'kô.	
Son, *n.*	Au mî lông.	Au *or* ô mi'lông.	Lit., child, male.
Sore, *n.*	Tâ'ra.	Tâ'ra.	
Sorrel (wild), *n.*	Ôg'yŭp.	....	
Sour, *a.*	Kû-nâm'a.	Kû-nâm'a.	
Sow (broadcast), *v.*	Kû.	Kû.	
Sow (with needle), *v.*	Ôm.	Ôm.	
Span, *n.*	Pin'gôp.	Pin'gôp.	
Span, *v.*	Pin'gôp gôp-kî.	Pin'gôp gôp-kî.	
Spark, *n.*	Ma'jêr.	Ma'jêr.	

English.	Shai'yâng Miri.	Abor.	Remarks.
Sparrow, *n.*	Pâk-shû'rông. Kûn-jŭjŭ'rî.	Pâk-shû'rông. Kûn-jŭjŭ'rî.	
Spear, *n.*	Gî'ding.	Gî'ding.	
Spear, *v.*	Gî'ding nik.	Gî'ding nik.	
Spear-grass, *n.*	Tâng'gôm.	Tâng'gôm.	
Speak, *v.*	Lû.	Pô.	
Spider, *n.*	Tâ-rûm-bû'tî.	Tâ-rûm-bû'tî.	
Spirit, *n.*	Ô'yŭ.	Ô'yŭ.	
Spleen, *n.*	Tûr'pui.	Tûr'pui.	
Spoon (wooden), *n.*	Ko'tûp.	Ko'tûp.	
Spittle, *n.*	Tâ'kir.	Tâ'kir.	
Spit, *v.*	Tâ'kir shûk-pâk	Tâ'kir shûk-pâk.	
Split small wood, *v.*	Tâk-kê.	Tâk-kê.	Holding in one hand and splitting with the other.
Split large do., *v.*	Pûk-kê.	Pûk-kê.	
Spread (as a mat, &c.), *v.*	Pû.	Pû.	Spread out *dhan* to dry in the sun is—"mur-lâtô-kâ."
Spunk (touchwood), *n.*	Mur'muin.	Mur'muin.	
Squint, *a.*	Tâ-lem'a.	Tâ-lem'a.	
Stand, *v.*	Dâk.	Dâk.	
Stand up things together, *v.*	Dâ-rûm.	Dâ-rûm.	Chiefly wood, but the word is also applicable to the standing up of other things if they rest one against another.
Stalk (*i.e.*, stem of plant), *n.*	Ât'kông.	Ât'kông.	
Star, *n.*	Tâ'kâr.	Tâ'kâr.	
Start (*i.e.*, to be disturbed suddenly), *v.*	Lôm'gê shû.	Lôm'gê shû.	
Step upon, *v.*	Sâ-tân.	Sâ-tân.	

Sting nettle, *n.*	Pa'jî ji'tâk. Pa'jî ji'mâng.	Pa'jî ji'tâk. Pa'jî ji'mâng.	Two kinds, one which stings and the other which does not.
Stick for stirring up rice while being cooked, *n.*	Pen'yô.	Pen'yô.	
Sticky, *a.*	Tâ-gâb'a.	Tâ-gâb'a.	
Stir food while in act of cooking, *v.*	Yŭ-lik.	Yŭ-lik.	
Stone, *n.*	Ur'ling.	Ur'ling.	Might be equally correctly written "aling." Abors send messages to the Miris by means of stones tied up in a little basket of bamboo. A stone thus tied up is called "lüpûr."
Stool, *v.*	Tai ê.	Tai ê.	
Stoop, *v.*	Tûng-kû.	Tûng-kû.	
Stranger, *a.*	Â'mî mâ-mem'a.	Â'mî mâ-mem'a.	
Strangle by hand, *v.*	Yŭm-shûr.	Yŭm-shûr.	
Strangle by rope, *v.*	Ôk-shûr.	Ôk-shûr.	
Straw, *n.*	Âm'rông.	Âm'rông.	
Stretch (as a human being), *v.*	Gur-jŭn.	Gur-jŭn.	
Strike (with hand), *v.*	Pî.	Pî.	
Strike (with wood, dao, &c.), *v.*	Pâ.	Pâ.	
Strong, *a.*	Tôr-nâm'a.	Tôr-nâm'a.	
Stumble, *v.*	Lê-shut.	Lê-shut.	
Substitute, *n.*	Â'lik.	Â'lik.	
Suck, *v.*	Mû.	Mû.	
Sugarcane, *n.*	Tâ'bât.	Tâ'bât.	
Sun, *n.*	Dâ'nyî.	Dâ'nyî.	
Sunshine, *n.*	Dâ'reng.	Dâ'reng.	
Sunshine, *a.*	Dâ-reng'a.	Dâ-reng'a.	
Sunrise, *n.*	Dâ'nyî ûk'shâ.	Dâ'nyî ûk'shâ.	
Sunset, *n.*	Dâ'nyî wâng.	Dâ'nyi wâng.	

English.	Shai'yâng Miri.	Abor.	Remarks.
Sweet, *a.*	Tî-nâm'a.	Tî-nâm'a.	
Sweet melon, *n.*	Ma'bâ.	Abors have none of this sort.	
Sweet potato, *n.*	Pâg'lî.		
Swollen, *a.*	Buî-nâm'a.	Buî-nâm'a.	
Sweep, *v.*	Pret *or* pret-buin.	Pret *or* pret-buin.	
Swift (as water), *a.*	Bin-nâm'a.	Bin-nâm'a.	
Swim, *v.*	Â'sî bâ.	Âsî bâ.	
Taboo, *n.*	Yôd'nâm.	Yôd'nâm.	
Tail, *n.*	Tâm'yô.	Tâm'yô.	
Take, *v.*	Lâ.	Lâ.	
Take oath, *v.*	Pê-shû. Bân-kî'to-kâ.	Pê-shû.	
Take away, *v.*	Bôm-kâ-lâng'kâ.	Bôm-kâ-lâng'kâ.	
Take out (of basket, cage, &c.), *v.*	Lâ-len.	Lâ-len.	
Take off clothes, *v.*	Pui-chû.	Pui-chû.	
Take off armlets, *v.*	Kôk.	Kôk.	
Take out earrings, *v.*	Shûg-len.	Shûg-len.	
Tall, *a.*	Bâ-dong'a.	Bâ-dong'a.	
Tarry (delay), *v.*	Toi-â-lâng kâ.	Toi-â-lâng'kâ.	
Taste (solids), *v.*	Dâkâng-kî.	Dâ kâng-kî.	
Taste (liquids), *v.*	Tung-kî.	Tung-kî.	
Teach, *v.*	No word. A particle "yîr" is used, and is attached to the root verbs; as— Ngôm lû-yîr'to-kâ=teach me to speak (lû=speak).		

Tear, *n.*	Mik'shi	Mîk'shî.	
Tear (by hand) *v.*	Pet.	Pet.	
Teaze (by tickling or pulling about), *v.*	Mû-rî.	Mû-rî.	
Teaze (by talking incessantly) *v.*	Lû-dîr-lû-sô.	Lû-dîr-lû-sô.	
Teaze (by constantly soliciting for things), *v.*	Kô-dîr-kô-sô.	Kô-dîr-kô-sô.	
Tell, *v.*	Lû.	Lû.	
Temple, *n.*	Kem'kem.	Kem'kem.	Lit., one *side* of face.
Ten, *a.*	Ê'ing.	Ê'ing.	
Testicle, *n.*	Et'tûm.	Et'tûm.	
That, *pron.*	Da.	Da.	
Thatching-grass, *n.*	Tâ'sê.	Tâ'sê.	
Them, *pron.*	Bû'lûm.	Bû'lûm.	
Then, *adv*	De'lô.	De'lô.	
There, *adv.*	A'lâ *or* Da'lâ.	A'lâ *or* Da'lâ.	
Therefore, *adv.*	Dê-pi'lâ.	Dê-pî'lâ.	
They, *pron.*	Bû'lû.	Bû'lû.	
Thief, *n.*	Dâ-pî-ô'na.	Dâ-pî-ô'na.	
Thieve, *v.*	Dâ-pi-ô.	Dâ-pi-ô.	
Thigh, *n.*	Â-rê-bî'ang.	Â-rê-bî'ang.	
Things (goods), *n.*	Âk-wâ'râng.	Âk-wâ'râng.	
Thin (animal), *a.*	Shâ-nâm'a.	Shâ-nâm'a.	
Thin (cloth), *a.*	Bâ-sôr'a.	Bâ-sôr'a.	
Thin (thread), *a.*	Rê-îka.	Rê-îk'a.	
Thirst, *n.*	Tü'ling.	Tü'ling.	
Thirsty, *a.*	Tü-ling'a.	Tü-ling'a.	
This, *pron.*	Sî *or* sî da.	Sî *or* sî da.	

English.	Shai'yâng Miri.	Abor.	Remarks.
Thorn, *n.*	Tâng.	Tâng.	
Thresh grain, *v.*	Âm yik.	....	Âm=paddy. Paddy is trodden out. Abors pull off the ears only when plucking.
Thread, *n.*	Ôn'nô.	Ôn'nô.	
Thread (needle, beads, &c.) *v.*	Ri-lîk.	....	
Throat, *n.*	Gürhî.	Gürhî.	
Threaten, *v.*	Mô-rid.	Mô-rid.	
Throw away things, *v.*	Yop-pâk.	Yop-pâk.	
Throw away or empty out water, *v.*	Pui-pâk.	Pui-pâk.	
Throw stone, *v.*	Ur'ling gê.	Ur'ling gê.	
Thumb, *n.*	Lâng'na.	Lâng'na.	
Thunder, *n.*	Dâ'muir muir'nâm.	Dâ'muir muir'nâm.	
Thunderbolt, *n.*	Tâng.	Tâng *or* Tâpui.	I can distinguish no difference between this word and the one for *thorn.*
Tickle, *v.*	Bâ'kîr kîr.	Bâ'kîr kîr.	
Ticklish *a.*	Âng-îr'a.	Âng-îr'a.	
Tick, *n.*	Tâpî.	Tâpî.	
Tie string, cane, &c., *v.*	Ngot.	Ngot.	
Tie up animal, *v.*	Rin.	Rin.	
Tie up hair, *v.*	Shûm.	Shûm.	
Tie (or bind) a man, *v.*	Yur.	Yur.	Tie hands (and) feet, and place him (there) "Â'lâk a'lê yurlâ ma'to-kâ."
Tighten, *v.*	So-git.	So-git.	

Tiger, *n.*	Sim'yâ.	Sim'yâ.	
Tired, *a.*	Bâ-gôr'a.*	Â-pê'a.	*Assam. word, Miris use no other.
Tobacco, *n.*	Dû'mâ.	Dû'mâ.	
Toe, large, *n.*	Lê'na.	Lê'na.	
Toe, others, *n.*	Lê'kê.	Lê'kê.	
Together, *adv.*	Lê-kô'pû.	Lê-kô'pû.	
Tongue, *n.*	Ai'yô.	Ai'yô.	
Tooth, *n.*	Î'pâng.	Î'pang.	My teeth are on edge (from eating anything tart)="Ngâka î-pâng'a î-kûm'ü".
Toothache, *n.*	Î'pâng kî-nâm'a.	Î'pâng kî-nâm'a.	
Top, *n.*	Tâ'lêng.	Tâ'lêng.	
Topsyturvy, *adv.*	Â'kin chû-mon'pû.	Âkin chû-mon'pû.	
Torn, *v.*	Bet'kâng.	Bet'kâng.	
Touch, *v.*	Ning-kî.	Ning-k.î	
Touchwood, *n.*	Mur'muin.	Mur'muin.	Got from a tree called "tâmâk" (Assam. "sêwâ"). The stuff is merely taken out and dried. It resembles cotton, and makes capital touchwood.
Trade, *v.*	Ka'rêt mô.	Ka'rêt mo.	
Transplant *v.*	Lê.	Lê.	
Tree, *n.*	Ur'sing â'muing.	Ur'sing â'muing.	*Names of trees.* Assamese. Miri. Gunkorai=âg'rûn. Pômâ=bân'jî. (*Cedrela toona*). Ooriam=tâk'kir. Bô'lâ=un'yŭm. Ô'lok=sî'lok. Ô'kon=ka'bâ. Mi'kai=tâ'pîl.

English.	Shai′yâng Miri.	Abor.	Remarks.
Trunk of tree, *n.*	Nur′ring, *or* Lur′ring.	Lur′ring.	
True, *a,*	Â′rü.	Ârü.	
Truly, *adv.*	Â-rô′pü.	Â-rô′pü.	
Try on clothes, *v.*	Ge-kî.	Ge-kî.	("Ge"=wear, "kî"=try, lit., count.)
Tumble,	*See* "Fall."		
Turn over anything, *v.*	Tâm-lât *or* tû-lât.	Tâm-lât *or* tû-lât.	
Twice, *adv.*	Lê′nyî.	Lê′nyî.	
Twins, *n.*	Ô-pem-shû′nâm.	Ô-pem-shû′nam.	
Twist ears, *v.*	Yê′rûng ê.	Yê′rûng ê.	
Two, *a.*	Nyî.	Nyî.	
Ugly, *a.*	Kân′kân mâng.	Kân′kân mâng.	Lit., pretty *not.*
Unable, *a.*	Î-lâ′mâ.	Î-lâ′mâ.	Lit., "î"=do, "lâ"=able, "ma"=negative particle not.
Uncle, paternal, *n.*	Yai, *or* Pai.	Yai, *or* Pai.	Father's eldest brother is called "yai," youngest "pai."
Uncle, maternal, *n.*	Nâ′na.		
Under (below), *adv.*	Rûm-kî′pü.	Rûm-kî′pü.	
Under, *n.*	Rûm-king′a.	Rûm-king′a.	
Understand, *v.*	Tât-ken.	Tât-ken.	("Tât"=hear, "ken"=know.)
Unfinished, *v.*	Pui-mâng-âdâ.	Pui-mâng-â′dâ.	(Lit., finished not still.)
Unripe, *a.*	Min mâ, *or* î-teng′a.	Min mâ, *or* î-teng′a.	("Min"=ripe, "mâ"=not.)
Upside down, *a.*	Kû-lûp′a.	Kû-lûb′a.	There are a lot of different words for different things.

Upstream.	Ling'in.	Ling'in.	
Upset (as a boat).	Pur-lik.	Pur-lik.	Roll to *r* in "pur" more like double *r*.
Urine, *n*.	Yê'sî.	Yê'sî.	Water is "âsî").
Vegetable, *n*.	Ô'ying.	Ô'ying	
Very, *adv*.	Ai-rû'pü.	Ai-rû'pü.	Miris also have a particle "rû" or "rûng," which is often used in lieu and sometimes as an intensive particle with "ai-rû'pü", as "It is very warm to day"="Sî'lô âng-kîr-rû'dâk." "I saw very many deer"="Sî mon'em bâ-jê-rûng'kâ kâ'tô.
Very well (all right), *adv*.	Châ.	Châ.	
Village, *n*.	Dâ'lûng *or* Dô'lûng.	Dâ'lûng *or* Dô'lûng.	
Vomit, *v*.	Bât.	Bât.	
Vulture, *n*.	Shâ'gûm.	Shâ'gûm.	
Waist.	Su loin.		
Wake, *v. i*.	Dâr.	Dâr.	
Wall (of house or side of boat), *n*.	Bâ'rê.	Bâ'rê.	
Wall lizard, *n*.	Pâ'tôt.	Pâ'tôt.	
Want, *v*.	Kô.	Kô.	
War, *n*.	Mî'mâk.	Mî'mâk.	
Warm (from sun), *a*.	Gû-nâm'a.	Gû-nâm'a.	
Warm (from fire), *a*.	Pâm'kyê.	Pâm'kyê.	
Wasp, *n*.	Tâ'gâng.	Tâ'gâng.	
Wash clothes, *v*.	Gâsôr nî.	Gâsôr nî.	
Wash face, *v*.	Mâ-mûk-shû.	Mâ-mûk-shû.	
Wash hands, *v*.	Lâ-shûk-shû.		
Wash body (bathe), *v*.	Ur-shû.	Ur-shû.	
Water, *n*.	Â'sî.	Â'sî.	

English.	Shai-yâng Miri.	Abor.	Remarks.
Water-melon, *n.*	Kû-mû'rûng.		
Wax, *n.*	Mût'kôn.	Mût'kon.	
Wear, *v.*	Ga.	Ga.	
Weed "dhan," *v.*	Rî'gû mô.	Rî'gû mô.	
Well (not ill), *a.*	Ai Kî mâ.	Ai Kî mâ.	
Wet, *a.*	Jü-jâng'a.	Jü-jâng'a, Yâ-pôm'a.	
What, *pron. rel.* and *interrog.*	In'qua.	In'qua.	
When? *adv.*	A-dî'lô.	A-dî'lô.	
Where? *adv.*	In-kâ'lâ.	In-kâ'lâ.	
Whence? *adv.*	In-kâ'lok.	In-kâ'lok.	
Which? *pron. rel.*	In'kâ.	In'kâ.	
Whistle, *v.*	Kô'yî î.	Kô'yî î.	
White, *a.*	Yâ-sing'a.	Yê-sing'a.	
White-ant, *n.*	Tâ'buin.	Tâ'buin.	
Who? *inter.* and *rel. pron.*	Sê'kô.	Sê'kô.	
Whose?	Sek'ka.	Sek'ka.	
Why? *adv.*	Kâ-pî'lâ.	Kâ-pî'lâ.	
Widower (also widow), *n.*	Tûm'bô.	Tûm'bô.	
Wide, *a.*	Bôrtê.		
Wife, *n.*	Mi'ang *or* Ma'ang.	Mî'ang.	A first wife is called "ê'pông," second ditto "ê'mê." If a man takes any more, there is no name for them!
Wind, *n.*	Ê'sâr.	Ê'sâr.	
Windy, *a.*	Ê-sâr'a.	Ê-sâr'a.	